AF445347

52 Weeks of Systematic Theology Workbook for Teens

A Complete Yearlong Guide with Weekly Questions, Reflection, and Real-Life Application

© Copyright 2026 - All rights reserved.

The content contained within this book may not be reproduced, duplicated, or transmitted without direct written permission from the author or the publisher.

Under no circumstances will any blame or legal responsibility be held against the publisher, or author, for any damages, reparation, or monetary loss due to the information contained within this book, either directly or indirectly.

Legal Notice:

This book is copyright protected. It is only for personal use. You cannot amend, distribute, sell, use, quote, or paraphrase any part, or the content within this book, without the consent of the author or publisher.

Disclaimer Notice:

Please note the information contained within this document is for educational and entertainment purposes only. All effort has been executed to present accurate, up-to-date, reliable, and complete information. No warranties of any kind are declared or implied. Readers acknowledge that the author is not engaging in the rendering of legal, financial, medical, or professional advice. The content within this book has been derived from various sources. Please consult a licensed professional before attempting any techniques outlined in this book.

By reading this document, the reader agrees that under no circumstances is the author responsible for any losses, direct or indirect, that are incurred as a result of the use of the information contained within this document, including, but not limited to, errors, omissions, or inaccuracies.

Welcome Aboard, Check Out This Limited-Time Free Bonus!

Ahoy, reader! Welcome to the Ahoy Publications family, and thanks for snagging a copy of this book! Since you've chosen to join us on this journey, we'd like to offer you something special.

Check out the link below for a FREE e-book filled with delightful facts about American History.

But that's not all - you'll also have access to our exclusive email list with even more free e-books and insider knowledge. Well, what are ye waiting for? Click the link below to join and set sail toward exciting adventures in American History.

Access your bonus here

https://ahoypublications.com/

Or, Scan the QR code!

Table of Contents

INTRODUCTION
Why Theology is for You

You might think theology is a word for dusty libraries and people with long beards. It sounds like a heavy chore or a school subject you did not sign up for. But here is a secret. **You are already a theologian.** Every time you think about why you exist, you do theology. Every time you wonder if God hears your prayers, you do theology. You have ideas about God, even if you never wrote them down.

Is theology just for old men in libraries? **No, it is for you, right now, in your real life.** The word comes from two Greek words: *Theos* (God) and *Logos* (Word or Reason). It simply means "thinking about God." This book helps you do that in an organized way. We call it **systematic** because we put these ideas in order. Think of it like a messy room. You might have your favorite shirts, your shoes, and your phone charger somewhere in the pile. Systematic theology is like putting those clothes in drawers and the charger on the desk. It helps you find what you need when life gets loud.

Why Should You Care?

You live in a world full of noise. Your friends have opinions. Social media has a million voices. Your teachers have their own views. If you do not know what you believe, you will move wherever the wind blows. Systematic theology gives you a solid place to stand.

- ✝ **It shapes your choices:** What you believe about God changes how you treat your friends.
- ✝ **It kills your fears:** Knowing God is in control helps when you feel anxious about the future.
- ✝ **It spots the lies:** When someone tells you something wrong about God, you will recognize it immediately.
- ✝ **It grows your love:** You cannot truly love someone you do not know.

How This Workbook Works

This is not a textbook you just read and toss aside. It is a guide for your daily life. Over the next **52 weeks**, we will look at the big pillars of faith. We start with the Bible and move all the way to what happens at the end of time.

Each week follows a simple pattern to help you get the most out of your study:

Section	What You Do
The Big Idea	Read a short, clear explanation of a specific truth about God.
Heart Check	Answer questions that help you see how this truth hits your own life.
Mind Map	Dig into a unique Bible verse to see exactly what God says.
Life Lab	Take one real action step to live out what you learned this week.

A Quick Note on "The Big Words"

Sometimes, theology uses big words. Words like *justification* or *sanctification* might seem tough at first. Do not let them stop you. These words are just labels for beautiful things God does for us. Think of them like the names of your favorite tools in a toolbox. Once you know what they do, you will be glad you have them.

We will use plain talk to get to the heart of these truths. You do not need a degree to get this. You just need a heart that wants to know the Creator.

The Goal of This Year

The point of this book is not just to fill your head with facts. Knowing facts about God is not the same as knowing God. You can know every stat about a pro athlete and never meet them. We want more than that. We want these truths to change the way you see yourself and the world around you.

By the end of these 52 weeks, you will have a clear map of your faith. You will speak about God with more clarity. You will feel more confident in your walk with Him. Most importantly, you will see how every piece of the Bible fits together into one great story.

Are you ready to see God for who He truly is? **Then let's get started.**

PART ONE
Trust God's Word

WEEK 1
Trust the Bible's Authority

"All Scripture is God-breathed and is useful for teaching, rebuking, correcting and training in righteousness," - 2 Timothy 3:16

The Big Idea: The Owner's Manual

Imagine you buy a brand-new, expensive drone. You take it out of the box, but you ignore the manual. You think you know how it works. You flip some switches, the motors spin, and then it crashes straight into a tree. Why did it crash? You did not listen to the person who built it.

Life works the same way. God created the universe. He created you. He did not leave us to guess how life works. He gave us a manual. We call it the Bible. When we talk about the **authority** of the Bible, we mean it has the right to tell us what to do. It has this right because God is the author.

Paul uses a specific word in his letter to Timothy: "breathed out." This means the words in your Bible came from the very lungs of God. He used human writers to pen the words, but He guided every single thought. Because it comes from God, it carries His weight. It is the final word on what is true and what is right. You can trust it more than your favorite influencer, your feelings, or even your own best guess.

Workbook: The God-Breathed Test

The Authority Scale

Look at the list below. Rate how much authority you give these things in your life from 1 (lowest) to 10 (highest).

- ✝ My best friend's advice: ____
- ✝ Social media trends: ____
- ✝ My gut feelings: ____
- ✝ The Bible: ____

The "Why" Question

If the Bible is "breathed out" by God, why does that make it more reliable than a science textbook or a history book? Write your answer in two sentences.

Heart Check: Fact vs. Feeling

Our culture tells us to "follow your heart." But the Bible says our hearts can trick us. Sometimes we feel like God is far away, but the Bible says He is near. Which one do you believe?

1. When you read something in the Bible that disagrees with how you feel, which one usually wins?

    ----

2. Does the idea of God having "authority" over your life make you feel safe or trapped? Why?

Mind Map: Breaking Down the Verse

Look at 2 Timothy 3:16 again. It lists four ways the Bible helps us. Match the word to its action:

Word	Action
Teaching	Showing us the right path to walk on.
Reproof	Showing us where we stepped off the path.
Correction	Showing us how to get back on the path.
Training	Showing us how to stay on the path.

Search and Find:

Pick one of those four actions. Find a time in the last month when the Bible did that for you. Briefly describe it.

Life Lab: The Manual in Motion

This week, find one "rule" or "instruction" in the Bible that you usually ignore because it feels hard or unpopular. (Hint: Look at how you talk about people or how you use your time).

The Task: For the next three days, follow that instruction exactly. Do not argue with it. Do not try to change it. At the end of the three days, write down if your life felt more or less "in line" than before.

☩ **My Bible instruction for this week:**

☩ **What happened?**

WEEK 2
Hear God's Voice in Nature

"The heavens declare the glory of God; the skies proclaim the work of his hands." - Psalm 19:1

The Big Idea: The Signature of the Artist

If you walk into a room and see a beautiful painting on the wall, you know someone painted it. You do not even have to meet the artist to know they are talented. They left their "signature" through the brushstrokes and the colors.

God did the same thing with the universe. Systematic theology calls this **General Revelation**. It is "general" because it is available to every person on earth, regardless of where they live or what language they speak. You do not need a library to know God exists. You just need to look up.

The stars, the oceans, and even the way your own DNA works all point back to a Maker. Nature is like a giant megaphone. It does not use words, yet it screams that God is powerful, creative, and loves beauty. When you stand on a mountain or watch a storm, you are seeing a small glimpse of His "handiwork." While nature cannot tell us how to be saved—we need the Bible for that—it tells us exactly who is in charge.

Workbook: Sky Watching

The Silent Shout Psalm 19 says that the sky "proclaims" things. Think about the last time you saw a sunset or a massive moon. What was that specific part of nature saying about God?

✝ **The Object:** (e.g., A thunderstorm)

✝ **The Message:** (e.g., God is powerful and huge)

____

____

General Revelation vs. Special Revelation We learn about God in two ways. General Revelation is nature. Special Revelation is the Bible and Jesus.

1. What is one thing you can learn about God *only* from nature?

   ____

   ____

2. What is one thing about God that nature *cannot* tell you?

   ____

   ____

Heart Check: General Revelation in My Backyard

Sometimes we get so busy looking at our phone screens that we forget to look at the "screen" God built.

1. Does looking at a massive galaxy make you feel small? Does that feeling make you feel scared or peaceful?

   ____

   ____

2. When you see something beautiful in nature, do you usually thank God, or do you just think it's a "cool coincidence"?

   ____

   ____

Mind Map: Breaking Down the Verse

Look at the words in Psalm 19:1 again.

✝ **"Declare":** This means to count or to recount. It's like the stars are constantly doing a presentation for us.

✝ **"Glory":** This refers to God's "weight" or His importance.

Read Romans 1:20:

> *"For since the creation of the world God's invisible qualities—his eternal power and divine nature—have been clearly seen, being understood from what has been made, so that people are without excuse."*

Based on this verse, why does God say people have "no excuse" for ignoring Him?

Life Lab: The Outdoor Observation

This week, your job is to go outside for ten minutes without your phone. Find a quiet spot. It could be your backyard, a park, or even just looking out a window.

The Task: Find three specific things in the natural world that prove God is an intentional Creator and not just "random luck."

1. Observation 1:

----

   o *What it proves about God:*

----

2. Observation 2:

----

   o *What it proves about God:*

----

3. Observation 3:

----

   o What it proves about God:

Prayer Prompt: "God, thank You for the way the world looks. Help me to see Your hand in everything I see today."

WEEK 3
See Why the Bible is True

"Sanctify them by the truth; your word is truth." -
John 17:17

The Big Idea: The Ultimate Standard

If you and a friend argue about how tall a door is, you do not just keep shouting at each other. You grab a tape measure. The tape measure is the "standard." It does not care about your opinion or your friend's guess. It just tells the truth.

Jesus tells us that God's Word is that tape measure for our lives. In His prayer, He did not say the Bible *contains* truth or *points* to truth. He said it **is** truth. This is a big claim. It means that everything the Bible says about history, God, and how we should live is 100% accurate.

We call this "inerrancy." This word means the Bible has no errors in its original form. Because God is the source of the Bible, and God cannot lie, the Bible cannot be false. It acts as a fixed point in a world where everyone seems to have their own version of "the truth." When you build your life on the Bible, you build on a foundation that will never crack or shift.

Workbook: The Truth Filter

The Source Test We hear thousands of claims every day. How do we know what to believe? Use the "Truth Filter" below. Write down a common phrase you hear at school or online. Then, look for what the Bible says about it.

✝ **What the world says:** (e.g., "Follow your heart.")

____

____

____

✝ **What the Bible says:** (e.g., Jeremiah 17:9 says the heart is deceitful.)

____

____

____

✝ **The Result:** Is the world's claim true or false?

____

____

____

True or False? Circle the correct answer based on what you learned today.

1. The Bible is true only when it talks about religious things. (**True / False**)

2. Because God is perfect, His written Word must also be perfect. (**True / False**)

3. Truth is something that changes based on how I feel. (**True / False**)

Heart Check: My Truth vs. The Truth

A common phrase today is "live your truth." This suggests that truth is different for every person.

1. How does it feel to know there is one solid truth that never changes? Does that feel restrictive or does it give you peace?

   ____

   ____

2. Is there a specific part of the Bible you find hard to believe is true? Why do you think that part is a struggle for you?

   ____

   ____

Mind Map: Breaking Down the Verse

Look at the word **"Sanctify"** in John 17:17. This word means "to set apart" or "to make holy."

How does the truth set us apart? If you know the truth, you will act differently than people who are just guessing. You will have a different kind of hope when things go wrong.

✝ **Question:** Why did Jesus want His followers to be "sanctified" by the truth? He wanted them to be distinct from the world around them. (Answered immediately).

____

____

Find the Contrast: Look up **Proverbs 14:12**. Compare it to **John 17:17**.

✝ Proverbs 14:12 says:

____

____

✝ What is the danger of following a path that "seems" right but isn't based on God's truth?

____

____

____

____

Life Lab: Spotting Lies in Culture

This week, be a "truth detective." Pay attention to the song lyrics you hear, the TikToks you watch, or the advice your friends give you.

The Task: Find one specific "lie" or "false claim" you encountered this week. A lie is anything that contradicts what God says in His Word.

1. **The Lie I heard:**

____

____

2. **Where I heard it:**

____

____

3. **The Bible's Truth that fixes it:**

____

____

Prayer Prompt: "Lord, help me to see through the lies of this world. Let Your Word be the light that shows me what is real."

WEEK 4
Find Everything You Need in Scripture

"Your word is a lamp for my feet, a light on my path." -
Psalm 119:105

The Big Idea: Enough for the Walk

Imagine you are hiking in the woods at night. The sun is down and you cannot see the trail. You do not need a massive spotlight that lights up the whole mountain. You just need a small lamp to see your next step. If you can see where to put your foot, you will not trip.

This is what theologians call the **sufficiency** of Scripture. It means the Bible contains every single thing we need to know God and live for Him. We do not need extra "secret" messages or modern prophets to tell us what God wants. He already said it. If it is important for your faith or your growth, it is in the Book.

Sometimes we want God to write a message in the clouds about which college to pick or who to date. We want the "whole map" of our future. But God gives us a lamp instead. A lamp only shows you the immediate space around you. As you take a step, the light moves with you. The Bible is enough because it gives us the wisdom to make those choices one step at a time.

Workbook: Path Finding

Is it Enough? Look at the list of "life needs" below. For each one, write down if you think the Bible gives you enough guidance to handle it.

✝ **Dealing with a mean friend:** (Enough / Not Enough)

____

____

✝ **Knowing how to get to heaven:** (Enough / Not Enough)

____

____

✝ **Handling your money:** (Enough / Not Enough)

____

____

✝ **Choosing a career:** (Enough / Not Enough)

____

____

The "Extra" Search People often look for truth in other places. Why do you think people check horoscopes or look for "signs" instead of reading the Bible?

____

____

____

Heart Check: My Lamp for This Week

Do you ever find yourself asking God for a sign? Most people do because we want to see the whole map. We feel like the Bible is too old or too general for our specific problems.

1. Do you trust that God has already given you all the answers you need for a holy life?

   ____

   ____

   ____

2. If you had to choose between a "feeling" and a Bible verse to make a big decision, which one would you pick?

   ____

   ____

   ____

Mind Map: Breaking Down the Verse

Look at the two parts of Psalm 119:105.

✝ **"Lamp to my feet":** This is for the immediate step. It prevents a fall _right now._

✝ **"Light to my path":** This is for the direction. it shows where the trail goes _overall._

Read 2 Peter 1:3:

*"His divine power has given us everything we need for a
godly life through our knowledge of him who called us by
his own glory and goodness."*

According to this verse, how much has God given us for life and
godliness?

____

____

____

Life Lab: Use the Light

Think of one decision you have to make this week. It could be small,
like how to spend your Friday night, or big, like how to talk to your
parents about a mistake.

The Task: Instead of asking your friends what they think, find one
Bible principle that applies to that choice. (Examples: Honesty, kindness,
putting others first, or working hard).

1. **The Decision:**

   ____

   ____

   ____

2. **The Bible "Light" (verse or principle):**

   ____

   ____

   ____

3. **The Action:** What will you do differently now that you have used
   the light?

   ____

   ____

   ____

Prayer Prompt: "God, thank You that I do not have to walk in the dark.
Help me to trust that Your Word is enough for every step I take."

PART TWO
Know Your Creator

WEEK 5
See God Everywhere

"Who can hide in secret places so that I cannot see them?"
declares the Lord. "Do not I fill heaven and earth?"
declares the Lord." - Jeremiah 23:24

The Big Idea: No Hiding Spots

Have you ever tried to hide from someone? Maybe you played hide-and-seek as a kid. Or maybe you tried to hide a bad grade from your parents. We often think that if we move to a different room or turn off the lights, we are alone. But with God, there is no such thing as a "secret place."

Theologians use the word **omnipresence**. This means God is fully present in all places at the same time. He is not spread out like a thin mist where a little bit of Him is in your room and a little bit is in the kitchen. He is 100% in both places. He is at your school, at your church, and even in the parts of the ocean where humans cannot go.

For some people, this feels scary. It means God sees the things you do when you think no one is looking. But for those who love Him, this is the best news ever. It means you are never truly alone. When you feel lonely in a crowded hallway or scared in the dark, God is right there with you. You do not have to travel anywhere to find Him.

Workbook: No Hiding Spots

The Presence Map

Think about your typical Tuesday. Write down three places you go and how knowing God is "filling" that space changes how you act.

1. **Place 1:** (e.g., The locker room)

    ____

    ____

    ____

o   *How it changes my actions:*

----

2. **Place 2:** (e.g., My bedroom at night)

----

   o   *How it changes my actions:*

----

3. **Place 3:** (e.g., A difficult class)

----

   o   *How it changes my actions:*

True or False?

1. God is bigger than the universe. (**True** / **False**)
2. If I go to a different country, I leave God behind. (**True** / **False**)

Heart Check: God is Here

Does the idea that God sees everything you do make you want to hide or make you feel safe?

1. What is one "secret place" in your life (a thought, a habit, or a place) where you have been trying to hide from God?

----

2. How does it feel to know He is already there and still loves you?

Mind Map: Breaking Down the Verse

Look at the question in Jeremiah 23:24. God asks if He does not "fill heaven and earth."

✝ **"Fill":** This implies that there is no "empty" space in the universe where God is absent.

Read Psalm 139:7–10:

"Where can I go from your Spirit? Where can I flee from your presence? If I go up to the heavens, you are there; if I make my bed in the depths, you are there. If I rise on the wings of the dawn, if I settle on the far side of the sea, even there your hand will guide me, your right hand will hold me fast."

Question: According to these verses, is there any physical or spiritual location where God is not present?

____

____

Life Lab: The Presence Practice

This week, pick a specific time when you usually feel stressed or alone.

The Task: For five minutes during that time, stop what you are doing. Speak out loud (or in your head) and say, "God, I know You are in this room with me right now." Talk to Him as if He is sitting right next to you, because He is.

✝ **When I did this:**

____

____

✝ **How it felt:**

____

____

WEEK 6
Rely on God's Unchanging Nature

"I the Lord do not change. So you, the descendants of Jacob, are not destroyed." - Malachi 3:6

The Big Idea: The Solid Rock

Think about how much your life has changed in the last three years. You probably look different. Your voice might have changed. Your favorite songs, your friends, and even your goals shift all the time. Humans change because we are growing, learning, or getting older.

God does not change. This is called **immutability**. He does not get "better" because He is already perfect. He does not get "older" or "weaker." His mood does not shift based on whether He had a good day. He is the same today as He was when He created the stars.

This is why we can trust His promises. If God said He loves you in the Bible, He still loves you now. He will not wake up tomorrow and change His mind about you. In a world where trends die in a week and friendships can end over a text, God is the only "Solid Rock" that stays the same.

Workbook: The Solid Rock

What Changes and What Stays?

List three things in your life that have changed recently. Then, list how God stays the same in response.

The Change	God's Unchanging Truth
(Example: My best friend moved away)	(God says He will never leave me)
1.	
2.	
3.	

The Identity Test

If God changed His mind, how would that affect your faith? Write one sentence.

____

____

____

____

____

____

Heart Check: Why We Need Stability

We live in a world that shifts constantly. This can make us feel shaky and anxious.

1. What is the most "unstable" part of your life right now?

   ____

   ____

   ____

2. How does Malachi 3:6 give you a sense of "gravity" in that situation?

   ____

   ____

   ____

Mind Map: Breaking Down the Verse

Look at the second part of Malachi 3:6: *"So you, the descendants of Jacob, are not destroyed."*

God is saying that because He does not change, He keeps His promise to protect His people. If He changed His mind about being merciful, we would be in big trouble.

Read Hebrews 13:8:

"Jesus Christ is the same yesterday and today and forever."

Question: If Jesus is the same forever, does that mean He is still doing the same kinds of things He did in the Gospels?

   ____

   ____

Life Lab: The Anchor List

This week, write down three specific promises from the Bible. (Example: "I am with you always" or "I will give you peace").

The Task: Every time you feel overwhelmed by a change this week, read your list. Remind yourself that even if your world is moving, the One who holds the world is not.

1. Promise 1:

   ____

   ____

2. Promise 2:

____

____

____

3. Promise 3:

____

____

____

WEEK 7
Praise God's Total Perfection

"Be perfect, therefore, as your heavenly Father is perfect." -
Matthew 5:48

The Big Idea: Better Than the Best

We use the word "perfect" a lot. We talk about a "perfect" score on a test or a "perfect" game in sports. But in reality, nothing on earth is truly perfect. Every car eventually breaks down. Every phone screen eventually cracks. Even the best humans make mistakes.

When we say God is perfect, we mean He is completely without flaw. He has no "bad side." He never has a bad idea. He never makes a mistake. He is the standard for everything good. This quality is often called His **Holiness.**

God's perfection is like a light so bright you cannot look directly at it. It highlights how much we need Him. We cannot reach His level on our own, which is why this verse is so challenging. He does not want us to just "try our best." He points us toward His own perfection. Since we cannot get there by ourselves, His perfection reminds us why we need a Savior to bridge the gap.

Workbook: Defining Holy

The Standard Check

Who do you usually compare yourself to? Is it a sibling, a celebrity, or a friend?

✝ **My usual "standard":**

____

____

____

____

✝ **What happens when I make God the standard instead?**

____

____

____

Word Study

"Holy" means to be set apart or "cut off" from what is common.

1. List one thing that is "common" in the world:

   ____

   ____

2. How is God the opposite of that common thing?

   ____

   ____

Heart Check: The Perfection Gap

Sometimes, thinking about God's perfection makes us feel guilty because we know we are not perfect.

1. Does God's holiness make you want to walk away from Him, or does it make you admire Him more?

   ____

   ____

2. How does it feel to know that a perfect God wants to have a relationship with an imperfect person like you?

   ____

   ____

Mind Map: Breaking Down the Verse

Matthew 5:48 says we "must be perfect."

Question: Does this mean God expects you to never sin again starting today? (No, it means He is calling you to a new direction and a new life through Jesus).

Read Isaiah 6:3:

> *"And they were calling to one another: "Holy, holy, holy is the Lord Almighty; the whole earth is full of his glory.""*

Question: Why do the angels repeat the word "holy" three times? In the Bible, repeating a word three times means it is the most important thing about that person.

Life Lab: The Excellence Challenge

This week, pick one task you usually do halfway; maybe cleaning your room, doing your homework, or practicing an instrument.

The Task: Do that task "perfectly" this week. Not to be a perfectionist, but as a way to honor the God who is perfect. See if doing things with excellence changes your attitude toward God.

✝ **The task I chose:**

____

____

____

✝ **What I learned:**

____

____

____

WEEK 8
Talk to Your Loving Father

"See what great love the Father has lavished on us, that we should be called children of God! And that is what we are! The reason the world does not know us is that it did not know him." - 1 John 3:1

The Big Idea: Family Talk

Theology can sometimes feel like studying a king from a long time ago. He is important, but He feels far away. But the Bible tells us that God is more than just a King or a Creator. He is a **Father**.

When you believe in Jesus, your status changes. You are not just a creature; you are an adopted child. This is a massive shift in how you talk to God. You do not have to use fancy words or follow a strict ritual. A child can walk right up to their father and ask for help.

God's love as a Father is not like human love. Human fathers can be grumpy or let us down. But God is the perfect Father. He listens perfectly. He provides perfectly. He disciplines us because He wants the best for us. Knowing God as your Father changes your prayer life from a chore into a conversation.

Workbook: Family Talk

Adoption Papers

In the ancient world, an adopted child had the exact same rights as a biological child.

1. List two "rights" you have as a child of God:

____

____

____

____

2. List one thing a child can tell a father that they wouldn't tell a stranger:

____

Name Tag

If you had to wear a name tag that described your relationship with God, what would it say? (e.g., "Employee," "Stranger," or "Child"). Why?

____

____

____

Heart Check: Living as a Child of God

Do you act like someone who belongs to God's family?

1. When you pray, do you feel like you are talking to a judge or a loving dad?

____

____

____

____

2. How does knowing you are "called a child of God" change how you feel about your own worth?

____

____

____

____

Mind Map: Breaking Down the Verse

1 John 3:1 starts with

"See what great love." We get the affirmation that we are children of God.

Question: "What does it mean knowing that we are children of God?

____

____

____

____

Life Lab: The Abba Prayer

This week, change the way you start your prayers.

The Task: For the next seven days, start every prayer by saying, "Father, I am your child, and I know You love me." Before you ask for anything, just spend one minute thinking about being part of His family.

✝ **Did your prayer feel different this week?**

____

____

____

____

✝ **Why or why not?**

____

____

____

____

WEEK 9
Recognize God Knows Everything

*"If our hearts condemn us, we know that God is greater
than our hearts, and he knows everything." - 1 John 3:20*

The Big Idea: Total Knowledge

Imagine if there was a giant screen above your head that showed every thought you had today. Every jealous thought, every lie, and every secret wish. You would probably want to run away and hide.

God already has that screen. This is His **omniscience**. He knows everything—past, present, and future. He knows the number of hairs on your head and the number of stars in the sky. He knows what you are going to say before you even open your mouth.

While this might feel like a lack of privacy, it is actually a source of great peace. You never have to worry about God "finding out" something bad about you and leaving. He already knew the worst parts of you when He chose to save you. You don't have to pretend to be someone else when you talk to Him. He knows the real you, and He loves the real you.

Workbook: Total Knowledge

The Knowledge Bank

List three things about you that only God knows.

    1.____

    2.____

    3. ____

God is Greater

The verse says God is "greater than our heart." When our heart tells us we are "trash" or "unlovable," God's total knowledge says otherwise.

✝ **What my heart says:**

____

____

✝ **What God knows:**

____

____

Heart Check: Privacy and Peace

Do you find it harder to believe that God knows your sins or that He knows your potential?

1. Does God knowing your future make you feel like you have no choice, or does it make you feel like your life is in safe hands?

   ____

   ____

   ____

2. How does God's knowledge help you when people misunderstand your intentions?

   ____

   ____

   ____

Mind Map: Breaking Down the Verse

Look at the phrase "he knows everything." There are no limits to His data.

Read Psalm 147:5:

> *"Great is our Lord and mighty in power; his understanding has no limit.."*

Question: If God's understanding is "beyond measure," can we ever surprise Him with our mistakes?

____

____

Life Lab: The Honest Review

This week, find a quiet place to sit with God.

The Task: Tell God something you have been trying to hide from Him. Even though He already knows, telling Him helps you realize there is nothing between you.

✝ What did you realize after being completely honest?

____

____

✝ How did it feel to know He wasn't surprised?

____

____

WEEK 10
Worship One God in Three Persons

"Therefore go and make disciples of all nations, baptizing them in the name of the Father and of the Son and of the Holy Spirit," - Matthew 28:19

The Big Idea: The Trinity Project

The **Trinity** is one of the most famous and most debated ideas in theology. It simply means that there is one God who exists in three distinct Persons: the Father, the Son, and the Holy Spirit.

Think of it like this: They are not three separate gods. They are also not just one God wearing three different "masks." They are three Persons who are all 100% God, yet they are all the same one God.

If this sounds hard to wrap your head around, that's okay! If we could explain God perfectly with a simple math equation, He wouldn't be much of a God. The Trinity shows us that God is a community within Himself. He has always had love and relationship between the Father, Son, and Spirit. When He created us, He invited us to be part of that relationship.

Workbook: The Trinity Project

One or Three?

Look at the roles of the Trinity below. Match the Person to their primary "work" mentioned in the Bible.

✝ **The Father:** (e.g., The one who sends the Son)

____

____

✝ **The Son:** (e.g., The one who dies on the cross)

____

____

____

✝ **The Holy Spirit:** (e.g., The one who lives inside us)

____

____

The Baptismal Name

In Matthew 28:19, Jesus says to baptize in the **"name"** (singular), not the **"names"** (plural). Why is that tiny detail so important for understanding the Trinity?

____

____

Heart Check: Mystery and Worship

Some people get frustrated that they cannot fully "solve" the Trinity.

1. Does it bother you that you cannot fully explain how God works? Why or why not?

____

____

2. How does the idea of God being a "community" change how you think about your own need for friends and family?

____

____

Mind Map: Breaking Down the Verse

Matthew 28:19 is often called the "Great Commission."

Read 2 Corinthians 13:14:

"May the grace of the Lord Jesus Christ, and the love of God, and the fellowship of the Holy Spirit be with you all."

Question: Paul lists all three Persons of the Trinity in this blessing. Why do you think we need the "work" of all three in our daily lives?

____

____

Life Lab: The Trinity Search

This week, look for the work of each Person of the Trinity in your life.

The Task: Each evening, write down one way you saw each Person at work.

✝ **The Father's Provision:** (Something He gave you)

✝ **The Son's Grace:** (A time you were forgiven or helped)

✝ **The Spirit's Guidance:** (A time you felt nudged to do the right thing)

PART THREE
See God in Action

WEEK 11
Marvel at How God Created All Things

"In the beginning God created the heavens and the earth."
- Genesis 1:1

The Big Idea: Out of Nothing

When you build a Lego set, you start with a box of plastic bricks. When you bake a cake, you need flour and eggs. Humans always create things out of *other* things. But when God made the universe, He started with a blank canvas. Actually, He started with no canvas at all.

Theology calls this *creation ex nihilo*. That is a fancy way of saying "creation out of nothing." God did not use spare parts from another galaxy. He spoke, and things that did not exist suddenly appeared. This shows us the sheer strength of His command.

Why does this matter for you? It means God owns everything. Since He made the atoms in your body and the stars in the sky, He has the right to say how they should work. It also means you are not an accident. You were a specific thought in the mind of God before the first star ever twinkled. You have a place in this massive universe because the Creator put you here on purpose.

Workbook: Out of Nothing

The Creator's Rights

If you write a song or paint a picture, you feel like it belongs to you. You get to decide what happens to it.

1. Since God created the whole world, what "rights" does He have over your daily life?

____

____

____

2. Name one part of your life you find hard to "hand over" to the Creator:

____

____

My Place in the Universe The universe is billions of light-years wide. Some people feel small and pointless because of that.

✝ **The Truth:** Does God's ability to create a huge universe make you feel ignored or does it make His focus on you feel more special? Explain why.

____

____

Heart Check: The Purpose of Beauty

God could have made the world gray and functional. Instead, He made it vibrant and wild.

1. When you see a beautiful animal or a cool landscape, what does that tell you about God's personality?

____

____

2. Do you live like you belong to God, or do you live like you are the one in charge of your own "creation"?

____

____

Mind Map: Breaking Down the Verse

Look at the very first four words of the Bible: *"In the beginning, God..."*

The Order of Things: Before time, space, or matter existed, God was already there. He is not part of the universe; He is outside of it.

Read John 1:3:

> *"Through him all things were made; without him nothing was made that has been made."*

Question: If nothing was made without Jesus, what does that tell you about His role in the very first moment of history?

____

____

____

Life Lab: The "Made on Purpose" Walk

This week, go for a walk and look at three different things: a plant, an animal (even a bug), and a person.

The Task: For each one, stop and remind yourself: "God spoke this into existence." Then, find one person this week who feels like they don't matter. Remind them (or yourself) that the King of the universe created them out of nothing for a reason.

✝ **Who did I encourage?**

____

____

____

✝ **How did it change my view of them?**

____

____

____

WEEK 12
Watch God Rule His World

"He is before all things, and in him all things hold together." - Colossians 1:17

The Big Idea: The Great Sustainer

Some people think God is like a clockmaker. They think He built the world, wound it up, and then walked away to let it run on its own. But the Bible says something different. God is not a distant observer. He is the **Sustainer**.

If God stopped thinking about the universe for one second, everything would fly apart. He keeps the planets in orbit. He keeps your heart beating. He ensures the seasons change. This part of theology is called **Providence**. It means God actively rules and cares for His creation.

Nothing happens by "luck" or "fate." Even the hard things in life are under His control. He works through the laws of nature and the choices of people to make sure His plans happen. You can sleep well at night because the One who holds your life together never takes a nap.

Workbook: The Great Sustainer

Who Holds My Life Together? When things go wrong, we often try to grab control.

1. What is one area of your life that feels "messy" or "falling apart" right now?

    ____

    ____

    ____

    ____

2. If Colossians 1:17 is true, is God holding that specific situation together too?   (Yes / No)

The Luck Myth We often say "Good luck!" to our friends.

✝ **Reflect:** If God is ruling every detail, does "luck" actually exist? How does knowing God is in control change how you feel about your future?

____

____

Heart Check: Anxiety vs. Providence

Anxiety usually comes from feeling like everything depends on you.

1. Do you feel more pressure when you think you are in charge of your life?

____

____

2. How does the truth that Jesus "holds all things together" take the weight off your shoulders?

____

____

Mind Map: Breaking Down the Verse

Look at the phrase _"in him all things hold together."_

The Glue of the Universe: Scientists look for "dark matter" or forces that keep atoms from flying apart. As a theologian, you know the ultimate "glue" is Jesus Christ.

Read Matthew 10:29-30:

> _"Are not two sparrows sold for a penny? Yet not one of_
> _them will fall to the ground outside your Father's care._
> _And even the very hairs of your head are all numbered."_

Question: If God cares about tiny birds and the hair on your head, is there any detail in your life too small for Him to manage?

____

____

____

____

____

Life Lab: The Control Hand-Off

Identify one thing you are currently worrying about. It could be a test, a sports game, or a conversation you need to have.

The Task: Write that worry on a piece of paper. Fold it up and put it inside your Bible at Colossians 1:17. Every time you start to worry about it this week, tap the Bible and say, "Jesus is holding this together, so I don't have to."

✝ **The Worry:**

____

____

____

✝ **How did it feel to leave it with Him?**

____

____

____

WEEK 13
Identify Different Kinds of Angels

"Are not all angels ministering spirits sent to serve those who will inherit salvation?" - Hebrews 1:14

The Big Idea: Invisible Helpers

Movies often show angels as chubby babies with harps or people with glowing wings. But the Bible describes them as fierce, mighty beings. They arc real, but they are usually invisible. God created them to be His messengers and servants.

Angels are not "ghosts" of dead people. They are a completely different type of creation. They do not get married, they do not die, and they have great strength. Their main job is to worship God and help His people.

Grasping the spiritual world helps you realize that there is much more to life than what you see. You might be walking to school alone, but the spiritual world is active all around you. God uses these "ministering spirits" to protect and guide those who follow Him. You are part of a story that involves both heaven and earth.

Workbook: Invisible Helpers

Angel Myths Check the boxes of the statements you think are true based on the Bible:

- ✝ [ ] People become angels when they die.
- ✝ [ ] Angels are created beings.
- ✝ [ ] Angels are meant to be worshipped by humans.
- ✝ [ ] Angels follow God's orders to help believers.

Knowing the Spiritual World How does knowing that God has a force of invisible servants help you when you feel scared?

____

____

Heart Check: Grasping the Unseen

Most of us live like only the physical world matters. We focus on our phones, our food, and our friends.

1. Do you ever think about the spiritual activity happening around you?

    ____

    ____

    ____

2. Does it comfort you to know that God sends help that you cannot see?

    ____

    ____

    ____

Mind Map: Breaking Down the Verse

Look at the phrase *"sent out to serve for the sake of those who are to inherit salvation."*

The Target of Their Service: Angels do not just fly around for fun. They have a mission. That mission is focused on *you*, the one who inherits salvation.

Read Psalm 91:11:

> *"For he will command his angels concerning you to guard*
> *you in all your ways;"*

Question: According to this verse, who gives the angels their orders? (This reminds us that we talk to God, not to angels, to ask for protection).

    ____

    ____

    ____

Life Lab: The Prayer for Protection

This week, when you feel nervous or walk into a difficult situation, remember Hebrews 1:14.

The Task: Ask God to send His protection. You don't need to see an angel to know God is acting. At the end of the week, write down a time you felt a strange sense of peace in a place where you should have been afraid.

✝ **The Situation:**

____

____

____

✝ **The Peace I felt:**

____

____

____

WEEK 14
Stand Against Evil Forces

"For our struggle is not against flesh and blood, but against the rulers, against the authorities, against the powers of this dark world and against the spiritual forces of evil in the heavenly realms." - Ephesians 6:12

The Big Idea: Winning the Daily Battle

Have you ever felt a sudden urge to lie? Or have you felt a wave of unexplained anger toward a friend? Sometimes, the struggle you feel is not just about your own bad mood. It is a spiritual battle.

The Bible is clear: we have an enemy. Satan and his fallen angels (demons) want to mess up God's plan and ruin your life. They use lies, fear, and temptation to trip you up. But here is the most important thing: they are already defeated. Jesus won the war when He rose from the dead.

Our job is to "stand firm." We don't fight *for* victory; we fight *from* victory. When you realize the real enemy isn't the person who was mean to you, it changes how you react. You stop fighting people and start using the spiritual tools God gave you to win the battle in your mind.

Workbook: Armor Up

The Real Enemy List a person you are currently frustrated with.

✝ **The Person:**

____

____

✝ **The Spiritual Lie:** According to Ephesians 6:12, is that person your real enemy?　　　　　　　　　　　　　　(Yes / No)

✝ How does this change how you will treat them tomorrow?

____

____

The Victory Mindset

If Jesus already won the war, why do we still have to "wrestle" every day?

____

____

____

Heart Check: The Battleground

The biggest battle happens in your thoughts. The enemy loves to tell you that you are a failure or that God is disappointed in you.

1. What is the most common "spiritual lie" you hear in your head?

    ____

    ____

    ____

2. How can you use the truth of the Bible to shut that lie down?

    ____

    ____

    ____

Mind Map: Breaking Down the Verse

Look at the list in Ephesians 6:12. It mentions rulers, authorities, powers of this dark world and spiritual forces of evil.

The Hierarchy of Evil: This shows us that the spiritual world is organized. The enemy has a plan, but God's plan is higher.

Read 1 John 4:4:

> *"You, dear children, are from God and have overcome them, because the one who is in you is greater than the one who is in the world."*

Question: Who is "he who is in you"? (The Holy Spirit). If He is greater than the enemy, do you ever need to live in fear of evil forces?

____

____

____

Life Lab: The Truth Shield

This week, identify one temptation or negative thought that keeps coming back.

The Task: Find one Bible verse that proves that thought is a lie. When the thought pops up, say the verse out loud. This is how you use the "Sword of the Spirit" to win the battle.

✝ The Negative Thought:

____

____

____

✝ The Truth Verse:

____

____

____

✝ How many times did you use it this week?

____

PART FOUR
Face the Problem of Sin

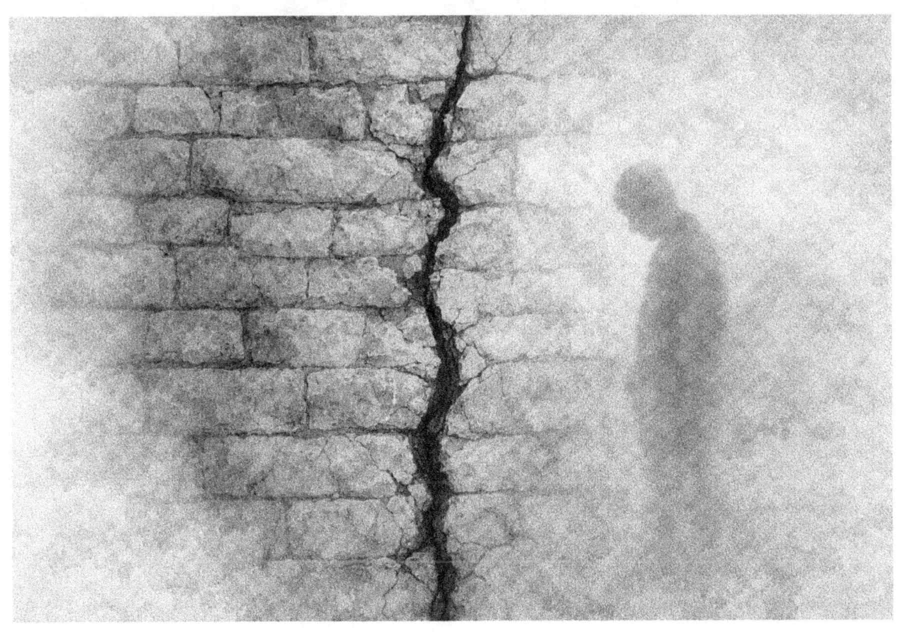

WEEK 15
Value Yourself as God's Image

The Big Idea: The Imago Dei and the Foundation of Human Worth

In a world that constantly tries to put a price tag on your soul, theology offers a radical counter-cultural truth: you possess an inherent, unchangeable dignity that was hard-wired into your being before you even took your first breath. This is the doctrine of the **Imago Dei** (Image of God).

To understand why this matters, we have to look at how the rest of the world assigns value. In our current culture, value is usually "earned" through performance, appearance, or social utility. If you are smart, you are "valuable." If you are athletic or famous, you are "valuable." This creates a fragile existence: if you lose your job, your looks, or your following, you lose your worth.

Theology flips the script. In Genesis 1:27, the Hebrew word for "image" is *tselem*, and for "likeness," it is *demut*. In the ancient world, a king would set up a *tselem* (a statue or image) of himself in a far-off land to show that he ruled there. As humans, we are God's "statues" on earth. We aren't God, but we are designed to represent His character, His creativity, and His authority.

This image-bearing isn't about what you *do*; it's about who you *are*. It means that every human, from the unborn child to the elderly person with dementia, from the billionaire to the person experiencing homelessness, carries the royal "stamp" of the Creator. When we talk about "valuing yourself," we aren't talking about "self-esteem" in the way pop psychology does. We are talking about recognizing that you are a divine masterpiece. To hate yourself is, in a sense, to criticize the Artist's work. To devalue others is to vandalize God's property.

Workbook

The God-Breathed Test

1. The Worth Audit Identify the three things you rely on most for your sense of "feeling good about yourself" (e.g., grades, dating life, sports, social media).

✠ **Source 1:**

____

____

✠ **Source 2:**

____

____

✠ **Source 3:**

____

____

Reflect: If one of these were taken away tomorrow, how would your view of your own value change? How does the doctrine of the *Imago Dei* act as a safety net for your identity?

____

____

2. The Mirror Exercise Read Genesis 1:27 three times slowly. Write down five specific attributes of God that you see reflected in human beings (e.g., God is a Creator, so humans are creative).

1. ____
2. ____
3. ____
4. ____
5. ____

Heart Check: Mirror Image

✠ Do you tend to view your "flaws" (physical or personality-based) as mistakes, or as part of a unique reflection of God?

____

____

____

✝ How would your daily interactions change if you saw a "miniature reflection of God" in every person you spoke to today, even the ones who annoy you?

____

____

Mind Map: Deep Dive into Genesis 1:27

The text says God created them "male and female." This is crucial. It suggests that neither gender can fully reflect the image of God on their own. We need the unique perspectives and traits of both to see the full picture of who God is.

Read James 3:9:

> *"With the tongue we praise our Lord and Father, and with it we curse human beings, who have been made in God's likeness."*

✝ How does James use the *Imago Dei* to argue against gossip and mean-spirited talk?

____

____

Life Lab: The Dignity Project

This week, your mission is to practice "Radical Dignity." **The Task:** Choose one group of people that society often overlooks (the elderly, service workers, people with disabilities, or even a specific student at school who is socially "invisible").

1. Find a way to show them they are valued. (Use their name, ask a thoughtful question, or offer a sincere thank you).

____

____

2. Record how acknowledging their "image-bearer" status changed the atmosphere of the interaction.

____

____

Observation:

____

____

____

WEEK 16
Respect the Differences in People

"There is neither Jew nor Gentile, neither slave nor free, nor is there male and female, for you are all one in Christ Jesus." - Galatians 3:28

The Big Idea: The Gospel as the Ultimate Equalizer

In the ancient world, the "walls" between people were towering. A religious Jew would not eat with a Gentile (a "Greek"). A free person had almost no social interaction with a slave. Men and women occupied vastly different worlds of power and opportunity. These weren't just "differences"; they were hierarchies.

When Paul wrote Galatians 3:28, it wasn't just a nice poem about being friends. It was a theological earthquake. Paul was arguing that while our physical, cultural, and social differences are real, they are **meaningless** when it comes to our standing before God. In the Kingdom of God, there is no "first-class" or "economy" seating.

This does not mean that we stop being "Jew or Greek" or "male or female." God loves diversity: He created it! But it means that our **union with Christ** is now our primary identity. If you are "in Christ," you have more in common with a believer halfway across the world who speaks a different language and lives in a different culture than you do with a non-believing neighbor who looks and acts exactly like you.

Theology teaches us that the Church is the one place on earth where the "boxes" should break. If our churches or friend groups only consist of people who look, think, and earn exactly like we do, we might be missing the power of the Gospel to unite what the world divides.

Workbook

One Body

1. Wall Identification Think about your current social circles (school, church, neighborhood). Identify three "invisible walls" that keep different groups of people from truly connecting.

1. ____

2. ____

3. ____

2. The Identity Ladder Rank these identities in order of importance to you (1 being most important):

☦ My Nationality/Ethnicity:

____

____

☦ My Family Name:

____

____

☦ My Hobbies/Talents:

____

____

☦ My Status as a Christian:

____

____

Reflect: If someone insulted your nationality, would you be more or less upset than if they insulted your faith? Why?

____

____

____

____

Heart Check: Breaking Down Walls

☦ Is there a specific group of people you find "hard to love" or "too different" to relate to?

____

____

✝ How does the truth that Christ died for them exactly as He died for you change your posture toward them?

____

____

Mind Map: Understanding "Union with Christ"

The key phrase in the verse is **"for you are all one in Christ Jesus."** Theology calls this "Union with Christ." Imagine a giant umbrella. Everyone standing under the umbrella stays dry. It doesn't matter if they are wearing a suit or rags, if they are tall or short. The "umbrella" (Christ) defines their reality.

Read Revelation 7:9:

> *"After this I looked, and there before me was a great multitude that no one could count, from every nation, tribe, people and language, standing before the throne and before the Lamb. They were wearing white robes and were holding palm branches in their hands."*

✝ If Heaven is diverse, why should the Church on earth strive to be the same?

____

____

Life Lab: The Bridge Builder

This week, purposely step outside your "social comfort zone." **The Task:** Initiate a conversation with someone who is different from you (different age, different background, or someone from a different social clique).

1. Listen to their story.

2. Find one thing you both share as human beings or as believers.

____

____

____

3. Write down one thing you learned about God's creativity through that person.

____

____

____

✠ **Learning:**

____

____

____

WEEK 17
Admit the Problem of Human Sin

"For all have sinned and fall short of the glory of God." -
Romans 3:23

The Big Idea: The Reality of the Broken Compass

We live in a "self-help" culture that tells us we are basically good people who just need better "tools" or "environment" to succeed. But theology is much more honest, and much more helpful. It tells us that we have a fundamental problem called **Sin**.

The Greek word for sin, *hamartia,* is an archery term. It means "to miss the mark." Imagine a target where the bullseye is God's perfect, holy character. No matter how hard we try, no matter how "nice" we are, we all miss. Some of us might miss by an inch (being a "good person"), and some might miss the target entirely (committing major crimes), but **everyone** misses.

But sin is more than just "breaking rules." It is a deep-seated rebellion. It is the desire to sit on the throne of our own lives. Theologians often speak of **Total Depravity**. This doesn't mean humans are as bad as they could possibly be (we are still capable of doing "good" things); it means that sin has touched *every part* of us, our minds, our emotions, our bodies, and our wills. Our "moral compass" is broken. Even our best intentions are often mixed with a little bit of selfishness.

Admitting this is the first step to freedom. If you think you're basically fine, you will never seek a Savior. You don't call an ambulance if you think you just have a common cold. Admitting the problem of sin is the "diagnosis" that makes the "cure" (Jesus) so beautiful.

Workbook

The Missing Mark

1. The Motivation Check

Think of the "best" thing you did this week (e.g., helping a friend, volunteering, being honest). Now, be brutally honest with yourself:

- ✝ Was any part of that action motivated by a desire to look good, feel superior, or get something in return?

  ____

  ____

- ✝ How does this help you understand why even our "good works" fall short of God's perfect glory?

  ____

  ____

2. The Standard Comparison

We usually compare ourselves to people "worse" than us to feel better.

- ✝ Who do you usually compare yourself to?

  ____

  ____

- ✝ What happens to your "goodness score" when you compare yourself to the perfection of Jesus instead?

  ____

  ____

Heart Check: Facing the Truth

- ✝ Does the phrase "I am a sinner" make you feel depressed or relieved? (Relief comes from knowing you no longer have to pretend to be perfect).

  ____

  ____

- ✝ In what area of your life are you most likely to "miss the mark" right now?

  ____

  ____

Mind Map: The Scope of "All"

Romans 3 is Paul's "legal closing argument" for the guilt of humanity.
Read Romans 3:10–12:

> *"None is righteous, no, not one; no one understands; no*
> *one seeks for God."*

✝ Why is it important that "not one" person is righteous on their
own? How does this destroy pride in the Church?

____

____

Life Lab: The Honest Inventory

This week, practice the spiritual discipline of **Confession. The Task:**
Spend five minutes each night this week being specific with God. Don't
just say "forgive my sins." Say, "Father, I was impatient with my sister
today," or "I lied to my teacher because I was afraid of looking stupid."

1. Write down how being specific about your "missed marks" makes
   God's grace feel more "real" by the end of the week.

____

____

✝ **Reflection:**

____

____

____

WEEK 18
Explain How Sin Started

"When the woman saw that the fruit of the tree was good for food and pleasing to the eye, and also desirable for gaining wisdom, she took some and ate it. She also gave some to her husband, who was with her, and he ate it." -
Genesis 3:6

The Big Idea: The Great Sabotage

If you've ever watched a movie where a character ignores a giant "Do Not Enter" sign only to trigger a global catastrophe, you have a small glimpse into Genesis 3. This chapter is often called **The Fall**, and it is the "Why" behind everything that is wrong with the world today. It explains why we have hospitals, graveyards, locks on our doors, and tears in our eyes.

To understand how sin started, we have to look at the psychology of the first temptation. Sin didn't start with a desire to be "evil"; it started with a desire to be **independent.** The Serpent (Satan) didn't approach Eve with a pitch for villainy; he approached her with a pitch for "self-improvement." He planted three specific seeds of doubt that we still struggle with every single day:

1. **Doubt of God's Word:** *"Did God actually say...?"* The first step toward sin is always questioning the clarity and authority of what God has commanded.

2. **Doubt of God's Character:** He hinted that God was holding out on them, that God was a cosmic killjoy who didn't want them to reach their full potential.

3. **Doubt of God's Judgment:** *"You will not surely die."* He promised there would be no consequences for rebellion.

When Adam and Eve ate the fruit, they weren't just eating a snack; they were declaring a coup. They were saying, "We don't want You to define right and wrong for us; we want to define it for ourselves." This is what theologians call **Original Sin**. Because Adam was the "Federal Head" (the representative) of the human race, his choice didn't just affect him. It "infected" the entire human stream. Like a drop of poison in a glass of water, sin entered the human nature, and we have all been born with that "bent" toward rebellion ever since.

Workbook

The First Choice

1. The Anatomy of a Temptation

Look at the three "hooks" mentioned in Genesis 3:6: *"Good for food"* (Physical appetite), *"Delight to the eyes"* (Material beauty), and *"Desired to make one wise"* (Social/Intellectual pride).

✝ Think of a temptation you faced this week. Which of these three hooks did it use?

____

____

____

✝ How did the enemy try to make God's command seem "too restrictive" in that Moment?

____

____

2. The Shift of Blame

Immediately after they sinned, Adam blamed Eve (and God!), and Eve blamed the Serpent.

✝ Why is it our first instinct to blame someone else when we "miss the mark"?

____

____

____

✝ What is the danger of never taking full responsibility for our own choices?

____

____

____

Heart Check: The "God Complex"

✝ Do you find yourself getting angry at God's rules because they feel like they are "stopping your fun"?

____

____

____

✝ How does remembering that God is a loving Father change how you view His "Do Not Enter" signs?

____

____

____

Mind Map: The Fallout

The Fall resulted in four broken relationships:

✝ **With God:** They hid from Him (Separation).

✝ **With Themselves:** They felt shame and nakedness (Inner Turmoil).

✝ **With Each Other:** They blamed and fought (Relational Conflict).

✝ **With Nature:** The ground was cursed with thorns (Environmental Decay).

Read Romans 5:12:

"Therefore, just as sin entered the world through one man, and death through sin, and in this way death came to all people, because all sinned—"

✝ If sin is a "hereditary disease," why is it impossible to fix it just by "trying harder" to be good?

____

____

____

____

Life Lab: Identifying the "Lies"

This week, pay attention to the advertising and social media posts you see.

The Task: Find one "message" that mimics the Serpent's lie ("You can have it all without God" or "You won't have to pay for this choice").

1. How is that message trying to sell you a "fruit" that will eventually lead to shame?

    ____

    ____

    ____

2. Write out a "Truth Counter" using a Bible verse you've learned.

    ____

    ____

    ____

✝ **The Lie:**

    ____

    ____

    ____

WEEK 19
See the Results of Disobedience

"For the wages of sin is death, but the gift of God is eternal life in Christ Jesus our Lord." - Romans 6:23

The Big Idea: The Economy of the Soul

In the world of finance, you have "earnings" and "bonuses." Your earnings (wages) are what you have a legal right to because of the work you did. A bonus (or a gift) is something given out of the goodness of the giver's heart. Paul uses this banking terminology to describe the most serious transaction in human history.

If we look at our lives as a "career of sin," the paycheck we have earned is **Death**. Theologians break this "death" down into three layers:

1. **Physical Death:** Our bodies decay and eventually die. This was never God's original design for humanity.

2. **Spiritual Death:** We are born "dead in our trespasses" (Ephesians 2:1), meaning our spirits are disconnected from the life of God. We are like a lamp that is unplugged.

3. **Eternal Death:** If we remain in our sin, we face eternal separation from God, the source of all joy, light, and love.

This sounds incredibly bleak, and it is. If the verse stopped at the word "death," we would be the most miserable people on earth. But the verse has a "But." In theology, the "Buts" of the Bible are where the hope lives.

God steps in and offers an alternative economy. He doesn't offer "better wages" (because we'd still fail to earn them). He offers a **Gift**. The word for gift here is *charisma*, which refers to a gift of grace that is totally unmerited. You can't work for it, you can't buy it, and you certainly don't deserve it. You can only reach out and take it. The "Result of Disobedience" is a debt we could never pay, but the "Result of Grace" is a life we could never earn.

Workbook

Wages and Gifts

1. The "What If" Scenario

Imagine if you were paid exactly what you "earned" for every thought, word, and action you had today.

- ✝ Would you be looking forward to your "paycheck" or would you be terrified of it?

  ____

  ____

- ✝ Why is the idea of "merit" (earning your way) actually a scary way to live when you understand God's holiness?

  ____

  ____

2. The Definition of Life

"Eternal life" isn't just about living forever (everyone lives forever somewhere). It is about *quality* of life: knowing God.

- ✝ What is one way your life feels "deader" when you are living in disobedience?

  ____

  ____

- ✝ What is one way you feel "more alive" when you are walking in the gift of God's grace?

  ____

  ____

Heart Check: The Pride of the Paycheck

- ✝ Do you ever find yourself trying to "pay God back" for your sins by being extra good?

  ____

  ____

- ✝ Why is "paying Him back" actually an insult to a free gift? (Hint: If someone gives you an expensive gift and you try to give them five dollars for it, how does that make them feel?)

  ____

  ____

Mind Map: Breaking Down the Verse

Feature	The Way of Sin	The Way of God
Method	Wages (Earned)	Gift (Free)
Source	My Effort	God's Grace
Result	Death (Separation)	Life (Union)
Location	In Self	In Christ Jesus

✝ If salvation were a result of works, what would the "vibe" of Heaven be like?

____

____

Life Lab: The Gift Practice

This week, give someone a gift that they absolutely did not earn. It could be doing a chore for a sibling who was mean to you, or buying a snack for someone who ignored you.

The Task: As you give it, think about Romans 6:23.

1. How did it feel to give something to someone who "deserved" the opposite?

    ____

    ____

2. How does this small act help you understand the heart of God toward you?

    ____

    ____

✝ **Action Taken:**

____

____

____

WEEK 20
Look for God's Covenants

"The days are coming," declares the Lord, "when I will make a new covenant with the people of Israel and with the people of Judah." - Jeremiah 31:31

The Big Idea: The Promise Keeper

In our world, we have "contracts." A contract says, "I'll do this if you do that, and if you fail, the deal is off." But God doesn't do contracts; He does **Covenants**. A covenant is a solemn, binding relationship where God binds Himself to His people. Even when we are unfaithful, God remains faithful because His own name and reputation are on the line.

The Bible is organized around several major covenants:

1. **The Noahic Covenant:** God promised never to destroy the earth with a flood again (Sign: The Rainbow).

2. **The Abrahamic Covenant:** God promised to make a great nation from Abraham and to bless the whole world through his offspring (Sign: Circumcision).

3. **The Mosaic Covenant:** God gave the Law (Ten Commandments) to show His people how to live holy lives (Sign: The Sabbath).

4. **The Davidic Covenant:** God promised that a King from David's line would rule forever (Jesus!).

The problem was that while God kept His side of these covenants, humans kept failing. We couldn't keep the Law on the stone tablets. So, Jeremiah 31 prophesies a **New Covenant**. This is the climax of the story. In this "New Deal," God does something radical: He doesn't just give us a list of rules; He gives us a **new heart.**

Instead of an external law that we have to work hard to obey, God puts His Spirit inside us. He changes our "want-to." We don't obey because we are afraid of a contract being canceled; we obey because we are in a love-relationship with a Promise Keeper. The New Covenant is "New" because it is based on what God does *for* us and *in* us, rather than what we do for Him.

Workbook

The New Deal

1. Comparison of Covenants

Consider the following five comparisons:

Old Covenant (Moses)	New Covenant (Jesus)
Written on Stone	Written on the Heart
Focus on "Thou Shalt Not"	Focus on "I Will" (God's Power)
Temporary Animal Sacrifices	Once-for-all Sacrifice of Jesus
Requires Human Perfection	Requires Faith in Christ's Perfection

✝ Which of these sounds more "restful" to you? Why?

____

____

✝ Why is it easier to follow a rule when it is "written on your heart" (something you love) rather than just a rule on a sign?

____

____

2. The Personal Promise

Jeremiah says, *"For I will forgive their iniquity, and I will remember their sin no more."*

✝ If God "remembers your sin no more," why do you keep bringing it up to Him?

____

____

Heart Check: Internal vs. External

✝ Are you currently living under the "Old Covenant" mindset, feeling like God is only happy with you when you check off your "holy to-do list"?

____

____

____

✝ How would your week change if you truly believed you were in a permanent, secure covenant with God that was signed in the blood of Jesus?

____

____

Mind Map: Breaking Down the Verse

Look at the phrase *"I will be their God, and they shall be my people."* This is the "Covenant Formula." It appears all through the Bible. It shows us that the goal of all theology is not just "information" but **belonging**.

Read Hebrews 8:6:

> *"But in fact the ministry Jesus has received is as superior to theirs as the covenant of which he is mediator is superior to the old one, since the new covenant is established on better promises."*

✝ What makes a promise "better" when it comes from God rather than a human?

____

____

Life Lab: The Covenant Audit

This week, look at your "prayer list" or the way you talk to God.

The Task: Identify one "contractual" thought you have (e.g., "God, if I read my Bible today, You have to give me a good grade on my test").

1. Replace that contract with a "Covenant" thought (e.g., "God, I'm reading my Bible to know You better, and I trust You with my test because You are my faithful Father").

____

____

2. Write down the shift in your anxiety levels after making this change.

____

____

✝ **The Result:**

____

____

PART FIVE
Follow Jesus Christ

WEEK 21
Believe Jesus is Fully God

"In the beginning was the Word, and the Word was with God, and the Word was God." - John 1:1

The Big Idea: The Word is God

If you want to understand the identity of Jesus, you have to start before the manger in Bethlehem. You have to start before time itself. John 1:1 uses a specific title for Jesus: **The Word** (in Greek, *Logos*). In the ancient world, the "Logos" was the reason, the logic, and the force that held the universe together. John tells us that this "Force" is a Person, and that Person is Jesus.

Theology calls this the **Deity of Christ**. This means Jesus isn't just a "mini-god," a great teacher, or a high-ranking angel. He is 100% Jehovah. He is co-eternal with the Father, meaning there was never a time when Jesus did not exist. He didn't "become" God; He has always been God.

Why does His deity matter so much? Because if Jesus is not God, He cannot save you. A mere human, no matter how "good" they are, cannot pay the infinite debt of sin against an infinite God. Only God can satisfy the justice of God. If Jesus is just a man, then His death on the cross was just a tragedy. But if Jesus is God, then His death was a cosmic rescue mission. When you look at Jesus, you aren't looking at a "version" of God; you are looking at God Himself in a way we can finally understand. He has the authority to forgive sins, the power to create life, and the right to be worshipped.

Workbook

Why His Deity Matters

1. The "Liar, Lunatic, or Lord" Dilemma C.S. Lewis famously argued that Jesus didn't leave us the option of calling Him just a "great moral teacher." He claimed to be God.

✝ If someone claims to be God but isn't, they are either a **Liar** (knowing they aren't God) or a **Lunatic** (thinking they are God when they aren't).

✝ Do you think Jesus' actions in the Bible (healing the blind, raising the dead, showing perfect love) fit the profile of a liar or a lunatic? Why or why not?

____

____

2. The Attributes Check List three things Jesus did in the Gospels that only God has the power to do.

    1. ____

    2. ____

    3. ____

Heart Check: Is He Your Lord?

✝ If Jesus is truly God, that means He has total authority over your life: your money, your relationships, and your future. Does that thought make you feel restricted or secure?

____

____

✝ When you pray, do you talk to Jesus as a "buddy" or as the "Word who was with God"? How can you balance both?

____

____

Mind Map: Breaking Down John 1:1

✝ **"In the beginning..."**: Jesus was already there. He is uncreated.

✝ **"...was with God"**: Jesus is a distinct Person from the Father.

✝ **"...was God"**: Jesus shares the exact same nature as the Father.

Read Colossians 2:9:

"For in Christ all the fullness of the Deity lives in bodily form,"

✝ What does "whole fullness" mean? Is there any "part" of God that Jesus is missing?

____

____

Life Lab: The Worship Shift

This week, your goal is to worship Jesus specifically as God. **The Task:** Spend 10 minutes listening to a worship song that focuses on the holiness and power of Jesus. As you listen, tell Him: "Jesus, I acknowledge that You are the Creator of the stars and the King of the universe."

> ✝ **How did it feel to shift your focus from what Jesus does *for* you to who Jesus *is*?**

WEEK 22
Believe Jesus is Fully Man

"And Jesus grew in wisdom and stature, and in favor with God and man." - Luke 2:52

The Big Idea: Walking in Our Shoes

It is one thing to believe God is "up there" in Heaven. It is another thing entirely to believe He had to learn how to tie His sandals. This is the doctrine of the **Incarnation** (which literally means "entering into flesh"). Jesus didn't just "pretend" to be a human; He truly became one.

Luke 2:52 is a vital verse because it shows us that Jesus went through the same process of growing up that you do. He didn't pop out of the womb knowing the entire history of the world in human language; His human mind had to grow in wisdom. He didn't stay the same size; He grew in stature (He went through puberty, got taller, and probably had "growing pains"). He felt hunger, He got thirsty, He became exhausted, and He felt deep, gut-wrenching grief.

Theology calls this the **Hypostatic Union**: Jesus is one Person with two natures—fully God and fully man. Why does this matter? Because a Savior who has never been hungry can't truly empathize with the starving. A Savior who has never been tempted can't truly help those who are struggling. But because Jesus became a man, He "gets it." He knows what it's like to be misunderstood by family, betrayed by friends, and physically exhausted. When you cry out to Him, you aren't talking to a distant computer; you're talking to someone who has walked in your shoes.

Workbook

Jesus Understands Me
1. The Human Checklist

Look at these human experiences. Find a story in the Gospels where Jesus experienced each one:

✝ **Exhaustion:** (John 4:6 - Resting by a well)

✝ **Grief:**

____

✝ **Anger:**

✝ **Physical Pain:**

----

2. The Sympathy Factor

Hebrews 4:15 says:

> *"For we do not have a high priest who is unable to empathize with our weaknesses, but we have one who has been tempted in every way, just as we are—yet he did not sin."*

✝ Think of the hardest thing you are going through right now. How does it change your prayer to know that Jesus has felt the human emotion behind that struggle?

Heart Check: The Relatable King

✝ Do you ever feel like God is "too big" to care about your "small" human problems?

✝ How does the fact that Jesus had a physical body (and still does!) make you feel closer to Him?

Mind Map: Why He Had to be Man

✝ **To be our Substitute:** Only a human can die in the place of humans.

✝ **To be our Example:** He shows us what a perfect human life looks like.

✝ **To be our Mediator:** He stands between God and man because He belongs to both worlds.

Read Hebrews 2:17:

> *"For this reason he had to be made like them,[a] fully human in every way, in order that he might become a merciful and faithful high priest in service to God, and that he might make atonement for the sins of the people."*

✝ If Jesus was missing even one part of being human (like having no human emotions), would He still be "like His brothers in every respect"?

____

____

Life Lab: The "Me Too" Prayer

This week, when you feel a strong emotion (sadness, frustration, or even joy), stop and tell Jesus about it. **The Task:** Instead of just asking Him to "fix" it, say: "Jesus, I know You felt this too. Thank You for understanding what this feels like."

✝ **What was the emotion?**

____

____

✝ **Did you feel more "heard" knowing He has experienced it?**

____

____

WEEK 23
Study Why Jesus Had to Die

"He himself bore our sins" in his body on the cross, so that
we might die to sins and live for righteousness; "by his
wounds you have been healed." - 1 Peter 2:24

The Big Idea: The Great Exchange

The Cross is the most famous symbol in the world, but many people don't understand the "mechanics" of what happened there. Why did a "good person" have to die such a brutal death? The answer lies in the **Great Exchange** (also known as *Substitutionary Atonement*).

Imagine you are in a courtroom. You are guilty of a massive crime, and the fine is $10 million. You have $0. You are about to go to prison forever. But then, the Judge Himself steps down from the bench, takes off His robe, and writes a check for the full $10 million. He pays your debt, and you walk free.

On the Cross, two things happened simultaneously. First, Jesus took all of your "bad" (your sins, your shame, your rebellion) and put it on His own shoulders. God treated Jesus as if He had lived your life. Second, Jesus took all of His "good" (His perfect obedience, His holiness) and gave it to you. Now, when God looks at you, He treats you as if you had lived Jesus' perfect life. This is why 1 Peter 2:24 says He "bore our sins in his body." He was our Scapegoat. He took the "wages of sin" (Death) so that we could receive the "gift of God" (Life). He didn't just die *for* us; He died *instead of* us.

Workbook

My Sins on His Shoulders

1. The Weight of Sin If sin is a "debt," how heavy does your debt feel on a scale of 1-10?

> ✝ Jesus didn't just pay for the "big" sins; He paid for every jealous thought and every white lie.

✝ How does it feel to know that the "bill" has been stamped **PAID IN FULL?**

----

2. The Scapegoat Imagery In the Old Testament, the priest would put his hands on a goat, "transferring" the sins of the people onto it, and then send it into the wilderness.

✝ How is Jesus like that goat?

Heart Check: Justice and Mercy

✝ At the Cross, God showed that He is perfectly **Just** (He didn't just "ignore" sin; He punished it) and perfectly **Merciful** (He took the punishment Himself).

✝ Does this make you fear God more, love Him more, or both?

Mind Map: The Results of the Cross

✝ **Propitiation:** God's anger at sin was satisfied.

✝ **Redemption:** We were "bought back" from the slave market of sin.

✝ **Reconciliation:** The "wall" between us and God was torn down.

Read 2 Corinthians 5:21:

> *"God made him who had no sin to be sin for us, so that in him we might become the righteousness of God."*

✝ If you have "become the righteousness of God," can you ever be "un-righteous" enough for God to stop loving you?

Life Lab: The Debt Cancellation

This week, write a list of 5 things you feel guilty about (past or present). **The Task:** Take a red pen and write **"PAID"** in big letters across the list. Then, rip the paper up and throw it away. Spend 5 minutes thanking Jesus that those 5 things no longer define who you are.

✝   **What did you feel as you threw the paper away?**

____

____

____

____

WEEK 24
Celebrate the Empty Tomb

"He is not here; he has risen! Remember how he told you, while he was still with you in Galilee:" - Luke 24:6

The Big Idea: Death is Defeated

If the story of Jesus ended at the Cross, it would be a beautiful story about a martyr, but it wouldn't be "Good News." The Resurrection is the "Receipt" of the Cross. It proves that the check Jesus wrote actually cleared. If Jesus had stayed dead, it would mean that sin and death were stronger than Him. But by walking out of the tomb, Jesus proved He is the Lord of Life.

Theology calls the Resurrection the **Vindication of Christ**. It is God the Father's way of saying, "Everything Jesus claimed is true!" It is the most important event in human history because it changes the "rules" of the universe. Before Easter, death was a one-way street. After Easter, death became a tunnel, it has an exit on the other side.

For the believer, the Resurrection isn't just a historical fact; it is a "now" reality. Because Jesus is alive, He can actually live *in* us through the Holy Spirit. We don't just follow the teachings of a dead man; we have a relationship with a living King. It also means that one day, we will be resurrected too. Death is no longer a monster to be feared; it is a defeated enemy that has lost its "sting." We can live with "Resurrection Power": the power to change, to overcome sin, and to hope even in the darkest moments.

Workbook

Living a Resurrected Life

1. The Evidence Trail The disciples went from being terrified and hiding in a locked room to being willing to die for their faith in a matter of days.

✝ What is the only explanation for that kind of radical change?

____

____

2. The Hope Anchor If Jesus can beat death (the biggest problem in the world), is there any "small" problem in your life that is too big for Him to handle?

✝ List one "dead" situation in your life (a broken friendship, a lost dream, a bad habit) that needs Resurrection Power.

____

____

Heart Check: The Living Presence

✝ Do you live your life like Jesus is a character in a book or like He is in the room with you right now?

____

____

✝ How does the Resurrection give you courage to face your fears today?

____

____

Mind Map: The Significance of the Resurrection

✝ **It validates the Gospel:** If He didn't rise, our faith is "useless" (1 Cor 15:14).

✝ **It guarantees our future:** He is the "Firstfruits, the first of many to be raised.

✝ **It gives us power:** The same power that raised Jesus lives in us.

Read Romans 6:4:

> *"We were therefore buried with him through baptism into death in order that, just as Christ was raised from the dead through the glory of the Father, we too may live a new life."*

✝ What does it look like to "walk in newness of life" at school or with your family?

____

____

Life Lab: The Resurrection Testimony

This week, look for "signs of life" in nature (a budding flower, a sunrise). **The Task:** Every time you see one, say: "Because He lives, I can live too." Then, find one person who is discouraged and share one reason why you have hope because of Jesus.

✝ **Who did you talk to?**

____

____

✝ **How did it change your own mood to focus on the Resurrection?**

____

____

WEEK 25
See Jesus Rule in Heaven

"The Son is the radiance of God's glory and the exact representation of his being, sustaining all things by his powerful word. After he had provided purification for sins, he sat down at the right hand of the Majesty in heaven." - Hebrews 1:3

The Big Idea: The Throne Room

Many people think of Jesus as a baby in a manger or a man on a cross. But where is He *now*? The Bible says He is "seated at the right hand of God." This is the doctrine of the **Session of Christ** (from the Latin word *sessio*, meaning "to sit").

In the ancient world, a priest never sat down in the Temple because his work was never finished: there was always another sacrifice to make. But Jesus "sat down" because His work of salvation is **finished**. He is not pacing the floors of Heaven worried about the world; He is resting in His victory. Sitting at the "right hand" is the position of ultimate authority and honor. It means Jesus is the true CEO of the universe.

What is He doing up there? He isn't just watching TV. He is **Interceding** for you. This is one of the most comforting truths in theology. Right now, Jesus is speaking to the Father on your behalf. When the enemy accuses you of your sins, Jesus points to His wounds and says, "That one belongs to Me." He is also ruling over the world, making sure that everything, even the bad things, works out for the good of His people. You don't have to panic about the news or the future, because your Best Friend is the one holding the gavel.

Workbook

Who is in Charge?

1. The Finished Work When Jesus said "It is finished" on the Cross, He meant it.

✝ Do you ever feel like you have to "earn" your way back into God's good graces after you mess up?

____

____

✝ How does the image of Jesus *sitting down* help you stop working so hard for God's approval?

____

____

2. The Intercessor Imagine Jesus in the Throne Room of God right now, mentioning your name to the Father.

✝ What is one thing you would like Him to "advocate" for you today?

____

____

Heart Check: Confidence in the King

✝ Does the world feel "out of control" to you right now?

____

____

✝ How does knowing Jesus is on the throne give you peace in the middle of chaos?

____

____

Mind Map: The Ascension and Session

✝ **The Ascension:** Jesus returned to Heaven in His physical body.

✝ **The Session:** He took the seat of authority.

✝ **The Intercession:** He prays for us constantly.

Read Romans 8:34:

> *"Who then is the one who condemns? No one. Christ Jesus who died—more than that, who was raised to life—is at the right hand of God and is also interceding for us."*

✝ If the King of the universe is your Lawyer, who can successfully bring a charge against you?

____

____

Life Lab: The Throne Room Prayer

This week, change the "posture" of your prayers. **The Task:** Before you ask for anything, spend 2 minutes picturing Jesus seated on a throne of light, ruling over every atom in the universe. Acknowledge His authority over your specific problems.

✝ **Did your problems feel "smaller" after picturing Jesus on His throne?**

____

____

WEEK 26
Expect Jesus to Return

"Men of Galilee," they said, "why do you stand here looking into the sky? This same Jesus, who has been taken from you into heaven, will come back in the same way you have seen him go into heaven." - Acts 1:11

The Big Idea: The King is Coming

History is not a circle; it is a line. It is headed toward a specific, climactic moment: the **Second Coming of Christ.** Just as surely as Jesus came the first time as a humble servant in a manger, He is coming a second time as a triumphant King on a white horse.

Theology calls this our **Blessed Hope.** Why is it "hope"? Because when Jesus returns, He is going to fix everything that is broken. He will wipe away every tear. He will end all injustice. He will destroy death once and for all. He isn't coming to "destroy the world," but to **restore** it. He is coming to make "all things new."

The Bible tells us to stay "ready." This doesn't mean we sit on a roof in white robes waiting for a cloud. It means we live with **Accountability**. We live as if our Master could return at any moment. This gives our lives urgency. We want to be found doing His work, loving people, sharing the Gospel, and being faithful, when He arrives. The Second Coming isn't something for Christians to be scared of; it is the "Happy Ending" we have been waiting for. It is the moment the King finally takes His rightful place, and we get to be with Him forever.

Workbook

Staying Ready

1. The Motivation Factor If you knew for a fact that Jesus was returning tomorrow at noon, what is the first thing you would change about how you spend your time today?

✝ Now, why not make that change today anyway?

____

2. The Restoration List: List three things in the world that break your heart (e.g., cancer, bullying, hunger)

   1. ____
   2. ____
   3. ____

✝ Now, write **"REPAIRED"** next to each one. This is what Jesus will do when He returns.

____

____

Heart Check: The Ultimate Reunion

✝ Are you excited for Jesus to return, or are you secretly hoping He waits so you can finish your bucket list?

____

____

✝ How does the promise of His return help you endure when life is hard?

____

____

Mind Map: The Nature of His Return

✝ **Personal:** It is Jesus Himself, not a "force."

✝ **Visible:** Everyone will see Him.

✝ **Sudden:** It will happen when people don't expect it.

✝ **Glorious:** He will be revealed in His full deity.

Read Revelation 22:20:

> *"He who testifies to these things says, "Yes, I am coming soon." Amen. Come, Lord Jesus."*

✝ Is "Come, Lord Jesus" a prayer you feel comfortable praying? Why or why not?

____

____

Life Lab: The "Maranatha" Morning

The early Christians used the word *Maranatha*, which means "Our Lord, come!" **The Task:** For the next seven days, the very first thing you say when you wake up is "Maranatha! Lord, come today." See if this "eternal perspective" changes how much you stress about small things throughout the day.

✝ **Reflection at the end of the week:**

____

____

____

PART SIX
Meet the Holy Spirit

WEEK 27
Discover the Spirit's Identity

"Then Peter said, "Ananias, how is it that Satan has so filled your heart that you have lied to the Holy Spirit and have kept for yourself some of the money you received for the land? 4 Didn't it belong to you before it was sold? And after it was sold, wasn't the money at your disposal? What made you think of doing such a thing? You have not lied just to human beings but to God." - Acts 5:3–4

The Big Idea: The Helper is God

One of the biggest mistakes people make in theology is referring to the Holy Spirit as "it." We often think of the Spirit as a battery pack for the soul or a "force" like something out of a sci-fi movie. But according to the Bible, the Holy Spirit is a **Person**. He has a mind, He has feelings (He can be grieved), and He has a will. Most importantly, as we see in Acts 5:3-4, the Holy Spirit is **God**.

In the story of Ananias and Sapphira, Peter makes a startling connection. He first accuses Ananias of lying to the "Holy Spirit," and in the very next sentence, he says, "You have not lied to man but to God." This is one of the clearest proofs of the Spirit's deity in the New Testament. He is the Third Person of the Trinity, equal in power, glory, and eternity to the Father and the Son.

Why does this identity matter? Because if the Holy Spirit were just a "force," He couldn't have a relationship with you. You can use a force, but you can only love a Person. Because He is God, when the Holy Spirit speaks to your heart or convicts you of sin, it is the Creator of the Universe communicating with you directly. He is called the **Paraclete** (the Helper or Counselor), which literally means "one called alongside." Imagine having the smartest, most powerful, most loving Being in existence walking right beside you at school, in your room, and during your hardest moments. That is the identity of the Holy Spirit. He is God with us, and He is God *in* us.

Workbook

Getting to Know the Spirit

1. Force vs. Person If you treat the Holy Spirit like a "force," you will try to "use" Him to get what you want. If you treat Him like a "Person," you will try to "know" Him.

✝ What is the difference between how you treat your phone (a tool) and how you treat your best friend (a person)?

____

____

✝ In what ways have you been treating the Holy Spirit like a tool rather than a Person?

____

____

2. The Trinity Check The Spirit is not "part" of God; He is fully God.

✝ Read **Matthew 28:19**. Why do you think Jesus tells us to baptize in the *name* (singular) of the Father, Son, and Holy Spirit?

____

____

Heart Check: The Grieved Spirit

✝ **Ephesians 4:30** tells us not to "grieve the Holy Spirit." You can't grieve a law or a force; you can only grieve someone who loves you.

____

____

✝ Is there a specific habit or attitude in your life right now that you feel might be "grieving" the Spirit of God?

____

____

Mind Map: The Spirit's Attributes

✝ **He Teaches:** (John 14:26)

✝ **He Testifies:** (John 15:26)

✝ **He Convicts:** (John 16:8)

✝ **He Intercedes:** (Romans 8:26)

Question: Which of these four roles do you feel like you need most in your life this week? Why?

____

____

Life Lab: The "Alongside" Walk

This week, try to practice the "Presence of the Spirit." **The Task:** Every time you transition from one activity to another (like walking from class to lunch), whispered a 5-second prayer: "Holy Spirit, thank You for being here with me."

✝ **Observation:** Did acknowledging Him as a Person change how "alone" you felt during the day?

____

____

____

WEEK 28
Watch the Spirit Work in the Bible

"Now the earth was formless and empty, darkness was over the surface of the deep, and the Spirit of God was hovering over the waters." - Genesis 1:2

The Big Idea: Breath of Life

The Holy Spirit didn't just show up at Pentecost in the New Testament. He has been active from the very first page of the Bible. In Hebrew, the word for Spirit is **Ruach**, which also means "breath" or "wind." Just as you cannot see the wind but can see what it moves, the Spirit is often invisible but His effects are massive.

In Genesis 1:2, we see the Spirit "hovering" over the chaos. The word for hovering is the same word used for a mother bird sitting on her eggs, waiting for life to break out. The Holy Spirit is the "Life-Giver." Throughout the Old Testament, the Spirit would "come upon" specific people to give them supernatural power for a specific task. He gave **Bezalel** artistic skill to build the Tabernacle; He gave **Samson** strength; He gave **David** the heart to lead.

However, in the Old Testament, the Spirit stayed *with* people, but He didn't always stay *in* them forever. The big change happened after Jesus rose from the dead. Because of Jesus, the Spirit now makes His home inside every believer. He moved from being a "visitor" to being a "resident." From creation to the prophets, and from the birth of Jesus to the birth of the Church, the Holy Spirit is the one who turns chaos into order and brings dead things to life. When you feel "formless and void" (empty or confused), the same Spirit who hovered over the waters of creation is ready to hover over your life and bring new life into your situation.

Workbook

From Creation to Now

1. The Wind Metaphor Read John 3:8:

> *"The wind blows wherever it pleases. You hear its sound, but you cannot tell where it comes from or where it is going. So it is with everyone born of the Spirit." Jesus compares the Spirit to the wind.*

✝ What are three ways the Holy Spirit is like the wind? (e.g., You can't see Him, but you can feel Him).

1. ____

2. ____

3. ____

2. Empowerment The Spirit gave people in the Bible "power" to do things they couldn't do on their own.

✝ What is one thing God has asked you to do that feels "too big" for your own strength? (Maybe forgiving someone, speaking up for what's right, or being patient).

____

____

✝ How does the Spirit's history of "hovering over chaos" give you hope for that situation?

____

____

Heart Check: The Life-Giver

✝ Does your spiritual life feel "formless and void" (boring or empty) right now?

____

____

✝ Are you trying to live for God in your own strength, or are you asking the *Ruach* (Breath) of God to fill your "sails"?

____

____

____

Mind Map: The Spirit's Timeline

- ✝ **Creation:** Hovering over the waters (Genesis 1:2).
- ✝ **The Prophets:** Speaking through men (2 Peter 1:21).
- ✝ **Jesus:** Descending like a dove at His baptism (Matthew 3:16).
- ✝ **The Church:** Filling believers at Pentecost (Acts 2:4).

Life Lab: The Nature Breath

The Task: Go outside and find a place where you can feel the wind on your face. Close your eyes for 60 seconds and think about Genesis 1:2.

1. Remind yourself that the same Spirit who breathed life into the universe is currently breathing life into your spirit.

   ____

   ____

2. Write down one thing you want the Spirit to "bring to life" in your heart this week.

   ____

   ____

- ✝ **My Prayer:**

  ____

  ____

WEEK 29
Accept the Spirit's New Life

"Jesus answered, "Very truly I tell you, no one can enter the kingdom of God unless they are born of water and the Spirit."' - John 3:5

The Big Idea: Born Again

When Nicodemus, a very religious man, came to Jesus in the middle of the night, he expected a conversation about rules or politics. Instead, Jesus told him he needed to be "born again." Nicodemus was confused—how can a grown man crawl back into his mother's womb? But Jesus wasn't talking about a physical birth; He was talking about a **Spiritual Regeneration.**

Theology teaches us that because of sin, our spirits are "stillborn." We are physically alive, but spiritually dead. We can't see God, we don't truly love God, and we are stuck in our own selfishness. The Holy Spirit is the one who performs the "miracle of the new birth." He is like a spiritual surgeon who takes out our "heart of stone" and gives us a "heart of flesh" (Ezekiel 36:26).

This "New Life" isn't something you can earn by being a good person. You didn't do anything to cause your first birth, your parents did! In the same way, you don't "cause" your second birth, the Holy Spirit does. He opens your eyes to see that Jesus is beautiful and that your sin is ugly. He gives you a new set of "wants." Suddenly, you *want* to pray, you *want* to help others, and you *want* to turn away from bad habits. This is the mystery of the Spirit's work. He changes you from the inside out so that you don't just "act" like a Christian; you actually *become* one.

Workbook

How the Spirit Changes My Heart

1. The Heart Transplant Imagine a heart of stone vs. a heart of flesh.

- ✝ A stone heart is cold, hard, and doesn't feel anything.
- ✝ A heart of flesh is warm, responsive, and can be hurt or happy.
- ✝ Where in your life do you still feel "stony" (unresponsive to God)?

____

____

2. The Evidence of Birth When a baby is born, it cries, it breathes, and it hungers for milk.

- ✝ What are some signs in your own life that the Holy Spirit has given you "New Life"? (e.g., Do you feel bad when you sin? Do you have a desire to understand the Bible?)

____

____

Heart Check: The Kingdom Door

- ✝ Jesus said this new birth is the *only* way to enter the Kingdom. Have you ever asked the Holy Spirit to give you this new life, or are you just trying to follow the rules?

____

____

Mind Map: The Order of Change

- ✝ **The Spirit Convicts:** Shows us our need for Jesus.
- ✝ **The Spirit Regenerates:** Gives us new life (Born Again).
- ✝ **The Spirit Seals:** Guarantees that we belong to God forever.

Read Titus 3:5: *"he saved us, not because of righteous things we had done, but because of his mercy. He saved us through the washing of rebirth and renewal by the Holy Spirit,"*

- ✝ If salvation is a "washing," what are some "dirty" parts of your past that the Spirit has cleaned?

____

____

Life Lab: The "New Cravings" Journal

This week, look for things you "crave" spiritually. **The Task:** Write down one moment this week where you felt a "tug" in your heart to do something good, to pray, or to stop doing something bad.

✝ **The Moment:**

____

____

✝ **Was it easy or hard to follow that tug?**

____

____

WEEK 30
Use Your Spiritual Gifts

"Now to each one the manifestation of the Spirit is given
for the common good." - 1 Corinthians 12:7

The Big Idea: My Part

When you become a part of God's family, the Holy Spirit doesn't just give you a "membership card"; He gives you a "tool belt." Every single believer is given at least one **Spiritual Gift**. These are not just natural talents (like being good at basketball); they are supernatural abilities given by the Spirit to help the Church grow.

Theology calls these the *charismata* (grace-gifts). The list in the Bible includes things like teaching, encouraging, giving, serving, leading, and many others. The most important thing to remember about your gift is the phrase "for the common good." Your gift isn't for you. It's not to make you famous or to make you feel superior. It's like a piece of a puzzle; it only makes sense when it is connected to the other pieces.

Imagine if your physical body were made of only eyeballs. You would see everything, but you couldn't walk, eat, or talk! A body needs different parts to function. The Holy Spirit is the Master Architect who decides which gift each person gets. Your job is not to be jealous of someone else's gift, but to find yours and use it. When you use your gift, you will feel a special kind of joy because you are doing exactly what you were "re-born" to do. You are a vital part of God's mission on earth.

Workbook

Finding My Unique Gift

1. Talent vs. Gift

- ✝ **Natural Talent:** Born with it (e.g., singing).
- ✝ **Spiritual Gift:** Given at spiritual birth (e.g., using your voice to lead people to God).

✝ What are two natural talents you have?

____

____

✝ How could the Holy Spirit use those talents as a "Spiritual Gift"?

____

____

2. The Body of Christ Read 1 Corinthians 12:12-27.

✝ If you feel like an "insignificant" part of the Church (like a pinky toe), what does this passage say to you?

____

____

Heart Check: The Comparison Trap

✝ Do you ever feel jealous of people who have "flashy" gifts (like preaching or leading)?

____

____

✝ How does knowing the Spirit chose *your* gift specifically for you help you stop comparing yourself to others?

____

____

Mind Map: Common Spiritual Gifts

✝ **Wisdom/Knowledge:** Understanding God's truth.

✝ **Faith:** Trusting God for big things.

✝ **Healing/Miracles:** Showing God's power.

✝ **Prophecy/Teaching:** Explaining God's Word.

✝ **Discernment:** Knowing right from wrong.

✝ **Service/Encouragement:** Helping and lifting others up.

Life Lab: The Gift "Test Drive"

This week, try on three different "hats" to see what your gift might be.

The Task:

1. **Serve:** Do a "behind the scenes" job without being asked. 2. **Encourage:** Write a note to someone who is struggling. 3. **Teach:** Explain a Bible verse to a younger sibling or friend.

✝ **Which one felt the most "natural" and gave you the most joy?**

____

____

____

WEEK 31
Follow the Spirit's Guidance

"So I say, walk by the Spirit, and you will not gratify the desires of the flesh." - Galatians 5:16

The Big Idea: Step by Step

Being a Christian isn't about following a map; it's about following a **Guide**. A map gives you all the directions at once, but a guide just tells you the next step. The Holy Spirit is our Guide, and Paul calls this process "Walking by the Spirit."

Every day, there is a "tug-of-war" inside you. On one side is your **Flesh**, that old part of you that wants to be selfish, lazy, or angry. On the other side is the **Spirit**, who wants you to be holy, loving, and patient. These two are in a constant battle. The side that wins is the side you "feed."

Walking by the Spirit means being sensitive to His "still, small voice." It's that little nudge you get to keep your mouth shut when you want to say something mean. It's that feeling of "check" in your spirit when you're about to watch something you shouldn't. As you learn to listen to these nudges and obey them, you become more like Jesus. It's not about being perfect all at once; it's about taking the *next* step in the right direction. If you fall down, the Spirit doesn't abandon you; He helps you up and says, "Let's take the next step together."

Workbook

How to Listen to God

1. The Tug-of-War Think about a decision you had to make today (even a small one).

✝ What did your "Flesh" want to do?

____

____

† What did the "Spirit" nudge you to do?

____

____

† Which one did you choose?

____

____

2. Learning the Voice How can you tell the difference between the Holy Spirit's voice and your own random thoughts?

† (Hint: The Spirit will *never* tell you to do something that goes against the Bible).

____

____

† Write down one verse that "fact-checks" a thought you had this week.

____

____

Heart Check: The Stillness Test

† It's hard to hear a guide if you're wearing headphones and screaming. Do you ever have "quiet moments" in your day where the Spirit can actually speak to you?

____

____

Mind Map: The Spirit's GPS

† **The Bible:** His primary way of speaking.
† **Prayer:** Where we listen and respond.
† **Other Believers:** Wise advice from friends.
† **Peace:** A sense of "rightness" in our hearts.

Life Lab: The "Yield" Practice

This week, practice the "Pause."

The Task: Whenever you feel a strong emotion (anger, jealousy, or temptation), stop and count to five. Ask: "Holy Spirit, what is the next step You want me to take?"

✝ **One time I paused this week:**

____

____

____

✝ **What happened?**

____

____

____

WEEK 32
Show the Fruit of the Spirit

"But the fruit of the Spirit is love, joy, peace, forbearance, kindness, goodness, faithfulness, gentleness and self-control. Against such things there is no law." -
Galatians 5:22–23

The Big Idea: Good Fruit

Have you ever seen an apple tree "trying" to grow apples? It doesn't grunt and strain and get stressed out. It simply stays connected to the roots, gets plenty of sunlight and water, and the apples grow naturally. This is how the **Fruit of the Spirit** works in your life.

Paul doesn't call these the "Works of the Christian." He calls them "Fruit of the Spirit." This means you can't "force" yourself to be more patient or more joyful. You can't just wake up and say, "I am going to have 10% more self-control today!" That is like taping an apple to a dead branch. True character change comes from the inside out.

As you "stay connected" to Jesus (through prayer, the Bible, and following the Spirit's guidance), these nine traits start to grow in you. People will notice that you don't get as angry as you used to, or that you're genuinely happy for others when they succeed. Notice that "Fruit" is singular, it's like one orange with nine slices. The Spirit wants to grow *all* of these in you. If you have "love" but no "self-control," the fruit isn't ripe yet. This week, we look at the "harvest" of a life that is led by the Spirit of God.

Workbook

What Kind of Tree Am I?

1. The Nine Slices Rank yourself from 1 (Needs Work) to 10 (Strong) on each slice:

- ✟ Love: ____
- ✟ Joy: ____
- ✟ Peace: ____
- ✟ Patience: ____
- ✟ Kindness: ____
- ✟ Goodness: ____
- ✟ Faithfulness: ______________________________________
- ✟ Gentleness: ____
- ✟ Self-Control: ______________________________________

2. Root Connection If you are low on "Peace," the answer isn't to "try harder to be peaceful." The answer is to "connect more to the Spirit."

- ✟ What is one way you can "water your roots" this week?

  ____

  ____

  ____

Heart Check: Artificial vs. Real

- ✟ Do you ever "fake" being a good Christian on the outside while feeling bitter on the inside?

  ____

  ____

  ____

- ✟ How does it feel to know that the Spirit is the one responsible for growing the fruit, and your job is just to stay connected to Him?

  ____

  ____

Mind Map: The Contrast

- ✟ **The Flesh produces:** Hatred, jealousy, fits of rage, selfish ambition (Gal 5:19-21).
- ✟ **The Spirit produces:** Love, joy, peace...

Question: If your life was a garden, which "crop" is currently taking up the most space?

____

____

Life Lab: The Fruit Inspector

The Task: Ask a parent, a close friend, or a mentor: "Which Fruit of the Spirit do you see growing in my life lately? And which one do you think I need more of?"

✝ **What they said I'm growing in:**

____

____

✝ **What they said I need more of:**

____

____

✝ **My prayer for this week:**

____

____

____

____

____

____

PART SEVEN
Walk the Path of Salvation

WEEK 33
Listen to God's Special Call

The Big Idea: The Invitation

Imagine you're at a crowded party and someone yells, "Pizza's here!" Everyone hears it. That's what theologians call the **General Call**. It's the gospel being preached to the whole world. But then, imagine your best friend leans in, whispers your name, and says, "Hey, I saved a specific slice just for you because I know it's your favorite." Suddenly, it's personal. You don't just hear the news; you respond to it. That is the **Effectual Call**.

Theology teaches us that because sin has made us "spiritually deaf," we can't hear God's invitation on our own. We need the Holy Spirit to act like a supernatural hearing aid. In Romans 8:30, Paul shows us a "Golden Chain" of God's work. It starts with God's plan (Predestination) and moves to God's voice (Calling).

This "Special Call" is the moment the Gospel stops being a boring story you hear in church and starts being the most important truth in your life. It's the moment you realize, "This isn't just about 'the world'; this is about *me*." God doesn't just send a mass email; He sends a personal invitation. Being "called" means that God has specifically chosen to open your eyes so you can see the beauty of Jesus. It's an invitation you can't help but want to accept because it's coming from the One who knows you best and loves you most.

Workbook

The Invitation

1. General vs. Specific

✝ **General Call:** Reading a Bible verse on a billboard.

✝ **Special Call:** Feeling like that specific verse was written exactly for what you're going through today.

✝ Can you think of a moment when the Bible suddenly "made sense" to you in a personal way? Describe it.

----

2. The Chain Link Look at the four "links" in Romans 8:30.

✝ Which link do you find the most comforting?

✝ Why is it important that **God** is the one doing the calling, rather than us finding Him on our own?

Heart Check: Hearing the Voice

✝ Do you ever feel like God is "interrupting" your life with His call?

✝ How does it feel to know that before you ever thought about God, He was already planning to call your name?

Life Lab: The Quiet Hour

The Task: This week, spend 15 minutes in total silence with your Bible open to Romans 8. Don't read for "information"; read to "hear."

1. Ask the Holy Spirit: "Lord, what are You calling me to see about Yourself today?"

2. Write down one thought that felt "personal" during that time.

____

____

____

✝ **The Call:**

____

____

____

WEEK 34
Turn Away from Sin

"Repent, then, and turn to God, so that your sins may be wiped out, that times of refreshing may come from the Lord," - Acts 3:19

The Big Idea: The U-Turn

In our culture, "repentance" sounds like a scary word used by people holding "The End is Near" signs. But in the Bible, the word for repentance is **metanoia**, which literally means "to change one's mind." It's a total 180-degree shift in the way you look at life.

True repentance has three parts:

1. **Mind:** You realize that sin isn't just a "mistake"—it's a rejection of God. You agree with God that your way was wrong.

2. **Heart:** You feel a genuine sorrow for your sin. Not just because you got caught, but because you realize you've hurt the One who loves you.

3. **Will:** You actually turn around. If you're walking toward a cliff and someone tells you to "repent," they aren't telling you to feel bad about the cliff; they're telling you to walk the other way.

Repentance is the "U-Turn" of the soul. It's saying, "I'm done trying to be my own god. I'm done chasing things that don't satisfy. I'm turning back to Home." The beautiful thing about Acts 3:19 is the result: your sins are "wipe out." In the ancient world, ink didn't have acid in it, so it sat on top of the paper. You could take a wet sponge and literally wipe the writing away as if it were never there. That is what God does when we turn back to Him. He doesn't just "ignore" the past; He erases it.

Workbook

The U-Turn

1. Regret vs. Repentance

✝ **Regret:** Being sad you got in trouble or that your life is messy.

✝ **Repentance:** Being sad you offended God and wanting to change for Him.

✝ Think of a time you were "sorry." Was it Regret or Repentance?

____

____

2. The Blotting Out If your life was a notebook and every sin was a sentence, what would it feel like to have God "wipe the page clean" today?

____

____

Heart Check: The Direction Check

✝ Is there one specific habit or attitude you've been "regretting" but haven't actually "turned away" from yet?

____

____

✝ What is stopping you from making that U-turn today?

____

____

Life Lab: The Direction Journal

The Task: Identify one "wrong direction" in your life (e.g., gossip, laziness, a specific secret sin).

1. Write down what "walking toward the cliff" looks like in that area.

____

____

2. Write down what "walking toward God" looks like in that same area.

____

____

3. Make the turn today by confessing it to God and taking the first
    step in the new direction.

    ____

    ____

    ____

✝ **The Change:**

    ____

    ____

    ____

    ____

WEEK 35
Trust God for Your Salvation

*"For it is by grace you have been saved, through faith—
and this is not from yourselves, it is the gift of God— not
by works, so that no one can boast." - Ephesians 2:8–9*

The Big Idea: No Boasting

If you could earn your way to Heaven, Heaven would be a very loud, annoying place. Everyone would be standing around bragging about how much money they gave, how many old ladies they helped across the street, and how many Bible verses they memorized. It would be a "Boasting Contest."

But theology gives us the doctrine of **Sola Fide** (Faith Alone) and **Sola Gratia** (Grace Alone). Salvation is not a trophy you win; it's a gift you receive. Think of it like this: You are drowning in the middle of the ocean. You can't swim. You're going under. Suddenly, a rescue boat pulls up and someone throws you a life ring. All you do is grab it.

The "grabbing" is **Faith**. The "life ring" and the "boat" are **Grace**. Even the strength to grab the ring is a gift from God. This is why we can't boast. We didn't build the boat, we didn't drive it to the middle of the ocean, and we didn't pay for the gas. God did 100% of the work. Our part is simply to trust that the life ring will hold us. Trusting God for salvation means stopping the "striving" and starting the "resting." It's admitting that you are $0 in the bank spiritually and that Jesus has paid your entire debt.

Workbook

Saved by Grace Alone

1. The Gift Analysis If you worked a job and got a paycheck, is that a gift? (Yes / No) Why?

____

____

✝ If salvation were a "paycheck," would you ever feel "safe"? (No, because you might get fired for a bad day).

____

✝ Why is a "gift" more secure than a "wage"?

____

____

2. Faith as an Empty Hand Theologians often describe faith as an "empty hand." It brings nothing to the table; it only receives.

✝ What are you currently trying to "bring to the table" to make God like you more?

____

____

Heart Check: The Pride Factor

✝ Do you find yourself looking down on people who aren't "as good" as you?

____

____

✝ How does Ephesians 2:8-9 crush that kind of pride?

____

____

Life Lab: The Grace Walk

The Task: Today, every time you do something "good" (like helping someone or praying), say to yourself: "This doesn't earn me anything. I'm already loved. I'm doing this because I'm grateful, not because I'm trying to get saved."

✝ **Did this change your motivation for doing good things?**

____

____

WEEK 36
Stand Right Before God

"Therefore, since we have been justified through faith,
we[a] have peace with God through our Lord Jesus
Christ," - Romans 5:1

The Big Idea: Court is in Session

Imagine you are standing in the highest courtroom in the universe. The evidence against you is overwhelming. The Prosecutor (Satan) has a list of every mean word, every selfish thought, and every secret lie you've ever told. The Judge is perfectly holy and cannot let sin go unpunished. You are 100% guilty.

Then, the Judge's Son steps forward. He shows the Judge His hands, hands that were pierced for your crimes. The Judge looks at the Son, then looks at you, and bangs the gavel. But He doesn't scream "Guilty!" Instead, He declares: **"JUSTIFIED."**

Justification is a legal term. It doesn't mean you "became perfect" in that moment. It means you were **declared** righteous. It's like a "legal exchange." God takes your sin and puts it on Jesus' account, and He takes Jesus' perfect record and puts it on your account. When God looks at you now, He doesn't see your mess; He sees the perfection of His Son. Because of this, you have "peace with God." The war is over. You aren't "on probation." You aren't "under suspicion." You are right with the Law because the Law has been satisfied by Jesus.

Workbook

Declared Not Guilty

1. Peace vs. Feelings Justification is a fact, but "peace" is often a feeling.

✝ Do you feel "at peace" with God right now, or do you feel like He is still mad at you?

____

____

✝ If the highest Judge has declared you "Not Guilty," does it matter if you still "feel" guilty? Why?

____

____

Heart Check: Facing the Accuser

✝ When you mess up, do you hear a voice saying, "God is going to get you"?

____

____

✝ How can you use Romans 5:1 to talk back to that voice of accusation?

____

____

Life Lab: The Courtroom Visualization

The Task: Spend 5 minutes today picturing that courtroom. See the gavel fall. Hear the word "Justified."

1. Write down one thing you've been feeling guilty about.

____

____

2. Draw a giant "X" over it and write "JUSTIFIED" next to it.

____

____

WEEK 37
Join God's Family as His Child

"The Spirit you received does not make you slaves, so that you live in fear again; rather, the Spirit you received brought about your adoption to sonship. And by him we cry, "Abba, Father." - Romans 8:15

The Big Idea: Abba Father

Justification is a legal status, but **Adoption** is a relational status. If you were a criminal and the Judge declared you "not guilty," that would be amazing. But what if the Judge then stood up, walked down from the bench, gave you a hug, and said, "Now, come home with me. I want you to be my child"? That is what God does for us.

In the Roman world, an adopted child had the exact same rights and inheritance as a biological child. Once you were adopted, your old debts were canceled and your new father became responsible for you. You didn't have to live in fear of being "kicked out" if you made a mistake. You were family.

Paul says we can now call God **"Abba."** This is an Aramaic word that is very intimate—like saying "Papa" or "Dad." It's the language of safety. A slave works because they are afraid of the master's whip. A child works because they love their father. Adoption changes our motivation. We don't pray or obey because we're afraid of being punished; we do it because we are part of the family business. You aren't just a "saved sinner"; you are a "beloved child." You have a seat at the table, a room in the house, and the Father's ear whenever you want to talk.

Workbook

Learning the Language of Adoption

1. Slave vs. Child

Attitude	The Spirit of Slavery	The Spirit of Adoption
Motivation	Fear of Punishment	Love for the Father
Prayer Life	Formal and Distant	Intimate ("Abba!")
Security	"Will I be kicked out?"	"I am forever a son/daughter."

✝ Which of these columns best describes your current relationship with God?

____

____

2. The Father's Heart What is one thing an earthly father does that helps you understand God as "Abba"? (Or, if you had a difficult relationship with your father, what is one thing you *wish* a father would do that God *actually* does?)

____

____

Heart Check: The Inheritance

✝ Do you live like someone who has a rich inheritance waiting for them, or like a spiritual orphan who has to scrounge for every scrap of love?

____

____

Life Lab: The "Abba" Morning

The Task: For the next three mornings, the first thing you say when you wake up is "Good morning, Abba." Don't use a formal prayer. Just acknowledge Him as your Dad.

✝ Did this change your "vibe" with God during the day?

____

____

WEEK 38
Grow More Like Jesus Every Day

"It is God's will that you should be sanctified: that you should avoid sexual immorality;" - 1 Thessalonians 4:3

The Big Idea: The Growth Spurt

Once you are justified (declared right) and adopted (made a child), God starts the lifelong project of **Sanctification**. This is the process of actually *becoming* in your behavior what God has already declared you to be in your status. If Justification is like being given a clean jersey, Sanctification is the hard work of actually learning how to play the game.

Unlike Justification, which happens in an instant, Sanctification is a "Growth Spurt" that lasts until the day you die. It is a cooperative work. God provides the power (Philippians 2:13), but you provide the effort (Philippians 2:12). It's like sailing, God provides the wind, but you have to hoist the sails.

Sanctification means that you are slowly but surely becoming more like Jesus. You're becoming more patient, less selfish, more honest, and more loving. It's often "two steps forward, one step back." You will still fail. You will still have "bad fruit" sometimes. But the overall direction of your life is toward holiness. You aren't who you *used* to be, even if you aren't yet who you *will* be. God is too loving to leave you in the mess He found you in. He is molding you into a masterpiece.

Workbook

Practicing Holiness

1. The Progress Report

Think back to who you were one year ago.

✝ Name one way you are more like Jesus today than you were then.

____

____

✝ Name one area where you still feel like you're "stuck" and need a growth spurt.

____

____

2. The Sail Metaphor Are you currently trying to "row the boat" (doing everything in your own power) or are you "hoisting the sails" (relying on the Spirit)?

✝ What does "hoisting the sails" look like in your daily life?

____

____

Heart Check: The Patience of the Gardener

✝ Does it frustrate you that you aren't "perfect" yet?

____

____

✝ How can you trust God's timing for your growth instead of getting discouraged?

____

____

Life Lab: The Habit Swap

The Task: Pick one "unholy" habit (like complaining or procrastination).

1. This week, try to "swap" it for a holy one (like gratitude or discipline).
2. Every time you feel the old habit kicking in, ask the Holy Spirit for the "wind" to do the new habit instead.

✝ **The Result:**

____

____

____

____

WEEK 39
Keep Your Faith Until the End

"being confident of this, that he who began a good work in you will carry it on to completion until the day of Christ Jesus." - Philippians 1:6

The Big Idea: Held Tight

One of the biggest fears new Christians have is: "What if I mess up so bad that God lets go of me? What if I lose my faith?" Theology answers this with the doctrine of the **Perseverance of the Saints**. But it might be better named the **Preservation of the Savior**.

You don't stay a Christian because you have a super-strong grip on God. You stay a Christian because God has a super-strong grip on you. Think of a father walking across a busy street with his toddler. The toddler is holding onto the father's hand, but the father is also holding onto the toddler's wrist. The toddler might trip, or get distracted, or even try to pull away, but the father isn't going to let go.

Philippians 1:6 is a promise. God is the one who "began" the work in you (Calling/Regeneration), and He is the one who will "complete" it. He is not a "quitter." He doesn't start a project and then get bored halfway through. If you are truly His, He will keep you. He will use trials to strengthen you, discipline to correct you, and grace to sustain you. Your salvation is as secure as God's ability to keep His promises. You can sleep well tonight knowing that the One who holds the stars also holds your soul.

Workbook

Why I Won't Fall Away

1. The Grip Test

  ✝ If your salvation depended 100% on your grip on God, how safe would you feel?

____

____

  ✝ How does it change your confidence to know He is holding your wrist?

____

____

2. The Completion Guarantee If God is a "Master Builder," does He ever leave a house half-finished?

  ✝ What is one trial you're facing right now that might actually be God "finishing" a part of your character?

____

____

Heart Check: Security vs. Laziness

  ✝ Does knowing God won't let go make you want to "sin more" because you're safe, or "love Him more" because He's so faithful? (True believers choose the second one!)

____

____

Life Lab: The Security Prayer

The Task: Tonight, before you go to sleep, read Philippians 1:6 aloud. Say: "God, thank You that You aren't finished with me. I trust Your grip more than mine."

  ✝ **Observation:** Did you sleep more peacefully after handing your "security" back to God?

____

____

____

____

WEEK 40
Know That Death is Not the End

"Yes, we are of good courage, and we would rather be away from the body and at home with the Lord." - 2 Corinthians 5:8

The Big Idea: Home Bound

We've reached the next step in our journey: **Glorification.** This is the moment when the "Order of Salvation" reaches its finish line. For the believer, death is not a "Game Over" screen; it's a "Level Up" screen.

Paul says that to be "away from the body" (to die) is to be "at home with the Lord." This is the **Intermediate State.** While we wait for our physical bodies to be resurrected at the end of time, our spirits go immediately into the presence of Jesus. No more sin, no more sadness, no more questions.

But the final hope isn't just "floating on a cloud." It's a **Physical Resurrection.** Just as Jesus rose from the dead with a real, touchable, perfect body, we will too. We will live on a "New Earth" where everything is restored. Death is like the "wardrobe" in the Narnia stories; it's just the door we walk through to get to the real world. We don't have to fear it, because Jesus has already walked through it and come back to tell us that the view on the other side is incredible. We are Home Bound.

Workbook

Losing the Fear of Death

1. The Definition of Home

 What makes a place feel like "home" to you?

____

____

____

✝ How does it change your view of Heaven to think of it as "Home" rather than a "cloudy city"?

----

2. The Final Upgrade If you could have a "Resurrection Body" with one specific "flaw" or "sickness" gone, what would it be?

✝ (Bible Fact: All of them will be gone!)

Heart Check: The Finish Line

✝ If you knew you were going to live forever in a perfect world with Jesus, how much would today's problems really matter?

✝ Are you ready to go Home, or is there still too much of "this world" holding you back?

Life Lab: The Eternal Perspective

The Task: Spend some time today looking at a sunset or a beautiful piece of nature.

1. Realize that this is just the "trailer" for the movie that is coming.
2. Say a prayer of thanks that death has lost its sting because of Jesus.

✝ **The Hope:**

PART EIGHT
Live as the Church

WEEK 41
Define What the Church Is

"Now you are the body of Christ, and each one of you is a part of it." - 1 Corinthians 12:27

The Big Idea: Not a Building

If you ask most people to describe "the church," they'll picture a building; maybe a cathedral with stained glass, a small country chapel, or a modern auditorium. But the New Testament writers would find that very confusing. For the first 300 years of Christianity, there were no "church buildings." People met in homes, in catacombs, or by rivers. This is because the Greek word for church, *ekklesia*, doesn't mean "architecture"; it means "an assembly of called-out people."

Theology teaches us that the Church exists in two "modes." First, there is the **Universal Church**. This is the spiritual reality of every believer who has ever lived, across every nation and every century. When you pray, you are joining a chorus of billions. Second, there is the **Local Church**. This is the specific "neighborhood" of believers you gather with. The Universal Church is the "family name," but the Local Church is the "home" where you actually eat, grow, and sometimes argue.

Paul uses the metaphor of the **Body of Christ** to show how this works. Think about how complex your physical body is. Your liver doesn't do what your lungs do, and your pinky toe has a completely different job than your brain. Yet, if your pinky toe is throbbing in pain, your whole brain is thinking about it. In the Church, diversity is not a problem to be solved; it's a design to be celebrated. We have different backgrounds, political views, and personalities, but we are held together by one "Head": Jesus Christ.

The Church is also described as the **Temple of the Holy Spirit**. In the Old Testament, God's presence lived in a stone building. In the New Testament, God's presence lives *in us* when we gather. This means that when the Church is healthy, people should be able to "see" God by watching how we love each other. If we are just a social club, we've missed the point. We are the "hands and feet" of Jesus, continuing the work He started 2,000 years ago.

Workbook

Not a Building | We are the Body

1. The "Organ" Assessment In a body, every part is necessary. If you were a part of the spiritual body, which one would you be today?

- **The Eyes:** You see needs others miss and have a vision for the future.
- **The Hands:** You are the first to volunteer for setup, cleanup, or manual labor.
- **The Heart:** You are deeply empathetic and spend your time encouraging the hurting.
- **The Knees:** You are a prayer warrior, supporting the body in secret.
- **My Choice, and why:**

____

____

2. The Problem of "Lone Ranger" Christianity Some people say, "I love Jesus, but I hate the Church."

- Based on the "Body" metaphor, can a hand survive if it decides it's "too good" to be attached to the arm?

____

____

- What is one thing you can only get from a group of believers that you *can't* get by yourself?

____

____

Heart Check: Loving the Mess

- Buildings are easy to maintain; people are difficult. Have you ever been hurt by someone in the church?

____

____

✝ How does knowing that *you* are also a "work in progress" help you show grace to the "messy" parts of the Church body?

____

____

Mind Map: The Church's Names

✝ **The Bride of Christ:** We are being prepared for a beautiful future with Him.

✝ **The Family of God:** We share the same Father and the same inheritance.

✝ **The Pillar of Truth:** We hold up the Gospel so the world can see it.

Life Lab: The Body Connection

The Task: This week, reach out to one person in your local church who is "different" from you (older, younger, or from a different background). Ask them: "How can I pray for you this week?"

✝ **Who did you reach out to?**

____

____

✝ **What did you learn about the "Body" from that conversation?**

____

____

WEEK 42
Lead Others with Grace

"Here is a trustworthy saying: Whoever aspires to be an overseer desires a noble task." - 1 Timothy 3:1

The Big Idea: Serving Well

In the corporate world, leadership is a ladder. You climb over people to get to the top so that others will serve you. In the Kingdom of God, leadership is a towel. You get down on your knees to serve others. This is the radical concept of **Servant Leadership**.

When Paul wrote to Timothy about "overseers" (elders) and "deacons," he didn't give them a list of business goals. He gave them a list of **Character Traits**. He cared about whether they were patient, whether they managed their families well, and whether they were "above reproach." Why? Because in the Church, you don't lead by *authority*; you lead by *influence*. If your life doesn't match your message, people won't follow you to Jesus; they'll run away from Him.

Grace-filled leadership means recognizing that you are a sheep before you are a shepherd. Even the pastor of the largest church is still just a person who needs the Gospel every morning. A grace-filled leader doesn't use "guilt" to get people to move; they use "inspiration." They are the first to admit when they are wrong, the first to sacrifice their own comfort, and the most consistent in showing mercy to the "strays" in the flock.

Whether you have a title in your church or you're just leading a small group of friends, your goal is the same: to be a **Pointer**. A good leader is like a signpost that says, "Don't look at me; look at Christ." If people are more impressed by the leader than by the Lord, that leadership has failed. We lead others with grace because that is exactly how Jesus led us, by laying down His life so we could find ours.

Workbook

What Makes a Good Leader?

1. The "Top 3" Traits Read **1 Timothy 3:1–13**. If you had to pick the three most important traits for a leader in today's world, which would they be?

1. ____
2. ____
3. ____

✝ Why is "not being a lover of money" so important for someone leading in the Church?

____

____

____

2. Leading from the Middle You might not be a "pastor," but you are a leader to someone (a sibling, a friend, a coworker).

✝ How can you "lead with grace" when that person makes a mistake?

____

____

____

Heart Check: The Title Trap

✝ Do you crave the "title" of leadership more than the "toil" of serving?

____

____

✝ If God asked you to serve "behind the scenes" where nobody would ever thank you, would you still do it with joy?

____

____

Mind Map: The Leader's Toolkit

✝ **The Bible:** Their only map.

✝ **The Towel:** Their primary tool.

✝ **The Knees:** Their secret weapon (prayer).

✝ **The Ear:** Their first response (listening).

Life Lab: The Foot-Washing Challenge

The Task: Identify someone in your life who "leads" you (a teacher, a boss, a pastor).

1. Write them a note of encouragement or do a small act of service for them this week.
2. Leadership is lonely; your "grace" toward them might be the very thing that keeps them going.

✝ **Who did you encourage?**

____

____

✝ **How did it feel to "lead the leader" with grace?**

____

____

WEEK 43
Participate in the Sacraments

"While they were eating, Jesus took bread, and when he had given thanks, he broke it and gave it to his disciples, saying, "Take and eat; this is my body." -
Matthew 26:26

The Big Idea: Symbols of Grace

Humans are sensory creatures. We learn by touching, tasting, and seeing. God knows this, so He didn't just give us a book; He gave us **Sacraments**. A sacrament is a physical act that points to a spiritual reality. In the Protestant tradition, we recognize two: **Baptism** and **The Lord's Supper** (Communion).

Think of **Baptism** as the "Wedding Ring" of the Christian life. Putting on a ring doesn't *make* you married, but it tells the world you are. Baptism is a public "burial." When you go under the water, you are saying, "The old, selfish version of me is dead." When you come up out of the water, you are saying, "I am a new creation in Christ." It is your official "initiation" into the family of God.

Communion is the "Family Meal." While baptism happens once, we take communion over and over again. Why? Because we are prone to "spiritual amnesia." We forget how much our sins cost and how much God loves us. When we eat the bread, we remember that Jesus' body was physically torn apart to heal our brokenness. When we drink the cup, we remember that His blood was poured out to wash our "permanent" stains away.

[Image showing the elements of Baptism (Water) and Communion (Bread and Cup) as 'Means of Grace']

Some traditions call these "Means of Grace." This doesn't mean the water or the juice has magic powers. It means that when we participate in faith, God uses these physical moments to nourish our souls. It's a time to "examine ourselves" (1 Corinthians 11:28), to make things right with our neighbors, and to feast on the truth that Jesus is enough. It is the highest point of Church unity, where the CEO and the homeless man eat the same bread and drink from the same cup, because they are equal at the foot of the Cross.

Workbook

Symbols of Grace | Baptism and Communion

1. The History of the Meal Read **Exodus 12:1–13** (The Passover) and compare it to **Matthew 26:26–28**.

- ✝ How is Jesus like the Passover lamb?

  ____

  ____

- ✝ Why did Jesus choose a *meal* to be the way we remember Him?

  ____

  ____

2. Personal Examination Before taking communion, we are told to examine our hearts.

- ✝ If you were to take communion right now, is there any "bitterness" or "unconfessed sin" you need to hand over to God first?

  ____

  ____

Heart Check: More Than a Snack

- ✝ Have you let communion become a boring ritual?

  ____

  ____

- ✝ How can you use those few minutes of silence during the service to actually "commune" (talk intimately) with Jesus?

  ____

  ____

Mind Map: The Two Ordinances

- ✝ **Baptism:** Focuses on my **New Identity** (Happens once).
- ✝ **Communion:** Focuses on my **Ongoing Relationship** (Happens often).

Life Lab: The "Table" Reflection

The Task: The next time your church offers communion, don't just take it.

1. Close your eyes and picture the night Jesus was arrested.
2. Think about one specific sin from your past week and "leave it" at the table.
3. As you swallow the bread/juice, say to yourself: "It is finished. I am forgiven."

✝ **How did this change your experience of the sacrament?**

____

____

____

____

WEEK 44
Worship God with Other Believers

"not giving up meeting together, as some are in the habit of doing, but encouraging one another—and all the more as you see the Day approaching." - Hebrews 10:25

The Big Idea: Better Together

We live in an era of "Individualistic Christianity." People say, "I don't need to go to church; I can worship God on a hike" or "I just watch sermons on my phone." While God is certainly in the woods and on the internet, there is something supernatural that happens when the **Local Church** gathers in one room that cannot be replicated in isolation.

The Bible uses the word ***Koinonia***, which we translate as "Fellowship." But *koinonia* is deeper than just having coffee and donuts. It means "shared life." When we gather, we are doing more than just listening to a lecture; we are "stirring one another up to love and good works" (Hebrews 10:24). We are like coals in a fire, when they are together, they stay hot. When you pull one coal out and set it on the side, it turns gray and cold in minutes.

Corporate worship is also a **Rehearsal for Heaven**. In Revelation, we see people from every tribe, tongue, and nation singing the same song. When we gather on Sunday, we are practicing for eternity. It's the one time in the week where we stop focusing on our "to-do" lists and focus on the "Done" list of Jesus.

Furthermore, gathering together provides **Protection**. The world is a loud place that is constantly trying to tell you that you are a failure, that you need more money to be happy, or that God isn't real. When you stand in a room of people singing the Gospel, you realize, "Oh yeah, that's right. I'm not crazy. This is true." We meet together to "re-calibrate" our hearts back to the truth.

Workbook

Better Together | Why We Gather

1. The Habitation of God Read **Matthew 18:20**. Jesus says when "two or three" are gathered, He is there in their midst.

✝ Does this mean God isn't with you when you're alone? (No).

____

____

✝ So what is "different" about His presence when we are together?

____

____

✝ **The Habits of the Early Church** Read **Acts 2:42–47**. List four things they did together.

1. ____

2. ____

3. ____

4. ____

✝ Which of these is missing from your life right now?

____

____

Heart Check: The Consumer vs. The Contributor

✝ Do you go to church to see what you can "get" (good music, good coffee, good feelings), or to see what you can "give" (encouragement, service, prayer)?

____

____

✝ How would your church change if everyone showed up with the goal of encouraging *one other person*?

____

____

Mind Map: The Goals of Gathering

✝ **Upward:** To worship and glorify God.

✝ **Inward:** To build up and encourage the saints.

✝ **Outward:** To be a witness to any seekers who might be watching.

Life Lab: The "Pew-Neighbor" Mission

The Task: This Sunday (or the next time you gather), don't just sit in your seat and wait for the service to start.

1. Look for someone who looks lonely or new.
2. Introduce yourself and ask, "How long have you been coming here?"
3. Listen to their story. You might be the "encouragement" that Hebrews 10:25 is talking about.

✝ **How did they respond?**

____

____

WEEK 45
Tell the World the Good News

"He said to them, "Go into all the world and preach the gospel to all creation." - Mark 16:15

The Big Idea: Gospel Sharing

Many Christians treat the "Great Commission" like the "Great Suggestion." We feel awkward, afraid of being "that person," or worried we won't have the answers to difficult questions. But **Evangelism** isn't a sales pitch; it is an act of love. If you knew a bridge was out and cars were heading toward the cliff, would you be "polite" and stay quiet, or would you wave your arms to save them?

Sharing the Gospel is simply **One Beggar Telling Another Beggar Where to Find Bread**. You don't have to be a theologian; you just have to be a witness. A witness doesn't argue the law; they just tell what they saw and heard. Your "Testimony" (the story of what Jesus has done for you) is the most powerful tool you have because no one can argue with your experience.

The key to sharing the King is **Making a Friend**. Jesus was known as a "friend of sinners." He didn't stand on a soapbox with a megaphone; He sat at tables and ate with people. He listened to their heartaches before He offered them hope. When we serve people and love them without an "agenda," we earn the right to be heard. Then, when the moment is right, we can say, "You know, I struggled with that same thing, and here is what helped me..."

Remember, you are not responsible for "saving" anyone; that is the Holy Spirit's job. Your only job is to be the messenger. If someone says "no," they aren't rejecting you; they are wrestling with God. Our goal is to leave people with a "better taste" of Jesus than they had before they met us.

Workbook

Making a Friend, Sharing a King

1. The Three-Part Story Practice telling your story in 60 seconds or less:

   ✝ **My Life Before:** (How I felt, what I chased)

   ✝ **The Turning Point:** (How I realized I needed Jesus)

   ✝ **My Life Now:** (The peace or purpose I have found)

----

2. Overcoming Fear Read **2 Timothy 1:7**.

   ✝ If God hasn't given us a "spirit of fear," where does the fear of sharing our faith come from?

   ✝ How does "love" (wanting the best for the other person) help push that fear out?

Heart Check: The Secret Cure

   ✝ Are you "keeping the cure to yourself" because you're afraid of what people will think of you?

   ✝ Who is one person in your life right now that desperately needs to hear there is hope?

Mind Map: The Evangelism "Flow"

✝ **Pray:** Ask God for an "open door."

✝ **Listen:** Find out where they are hurting.

✝ **Eat:** Spend time with them in "normal" life.

✝ **Speak:** Share how Jesus meets that specific hurt.

Life Lab: The "Open Door" Prayer

The Task: Every morning this week, pray this simple prayer: "Lord, give me one opportunity today to show or tell someone about Your love."

1. Keep your eyes open!
2. It might be someone like a neighbor needing help with groceries.

✝ **Did an opportunity show up?**

____

- -

✝ **What happened?**

____

- -

WEEK 46
Serve Your Neighbors with Love

"You, my brothers and sisters, were called to be free. But do not use your freedom to indulge the flesh[a]; rather, serve one another humbly in love." - Galatians 5:13

The Big Idea: Hands and Feet

The Gospel is a "Free Gift," but it should never make us "Lazy." In fact, the more we realize how much God has served us, the more we should want to serve others. This is the difference between "Religious Rules" and "Gospel Service." Religion says, "I serve so God will like me." The Gospel says, "God loves me, so I *get* to serve others!"

When we talk about "neighboring," we are talking about anyone who is in your path with a need. In the Parable of the **Good Samaritan**, Jesus showed that our "neighbor" isn't just the person who looks like us or goes to our church. It might even be our "enemy." Serving with love means we don't ask, "Do they deserve my help?" but rather, "How can I reflect Jesus to them?"

This is where the Church becomes the **Hands and Feet** of Jesus. In the first few centuries, the Church grew because Christians were the only ones who stayed in cities to care for the sick during plagues. They were the ones who rescued abandoned infants. Today, we serve by being the best employees, the kindest neighbors, and the most generous people in our communities.

Service is the "Apologetic" (the defense) of the Christian faith. People can argue with your theology, but it's very hard to argue with a group of people who are genuinely cleaning up their neighborhood, feeding the hungry, and showing up for people in their darkest hours. When we serve, we aren't just doing "good works"; we are making the invisible God visible to a watching world.

Workbook

Hands and Feet | My Service Plan

1. The "Neighbor" Audit Think of the physical people who live on your street or work in your immediate area.

✝ Do you know their names?

____

____

✝ What is one practical need you've noticed in their lives lately? (Maybe they're lonely, stressed, or sick).

____

____

2. Freedom to Serve Read **Galatians 5:13**.

✝ What does it mean to use your freedom as an "opportunity for the flesh"?

____

____

✝ How does being "set free from sin" actually make you *better* at serving others?

____

____

Heart Check: The Lowly Tasks

✝ Are you willing to do the "dirty work" (taking out the trash, cleaning the toilets, listening to a repetitive story) without getting any credit?

____

____

✝ How can you serve your family members this week as if you were serving Jesus Himself?

____

____

Mind Map: Three Levels of Service

✝ **Spontaneous:** Helping someone in the moment (holding a door, a kind word).

✝ **Planned:** Volunteering at a local ministry or nonprofit.

✝ **Systemic:** Working to fix the "root causes" of problems in your city.

Life Lab: The Secret Service

The Task: This week, do one "Secret Service."

1. Perform an act of kindness for a neighbor or friend, but do it in a way where they will *never* know it was you.

2. Pay for the person's coffee behind you, clean up a shared space, or leave an anonymous gift.

3. Enjoy the "secret" between you and God.

✝ **What did you do?**

____

____

✝ **How did it feel to not get the credit?**

____

____

PART NINE
Look at the Future

WEEK 47
Prepare for Christ's Second Coming

The Big Idea: Maranatha

The very last prayer in the Bible isn't a request for health, wealth, or a better life. It is a three-word cry: *"Come, Lord Jesus!"* In the original language, this is **Maranatha.** For the early Christians, this wasn't just a theological fact; it was a heartbeat. They lived with the constant expectation that Jesus could return at any moment to set the world right.

Theology speaks of Christ's return as the **Second Coming.** While His first coming was in humility, as a baby in a manger, coming to suffer and save, His second coming will be in glory. He won't come as a Lamb, but as a Lion. He won't come to be judged, but to judge. He won't come to die, but to reign. This is the "Great Hope" of the Church.

Living in light of the Second Coming creates a tension theologians call the **"Already and Not Yet."** We *already* have salvation, but we do *not yet* have our perfect bodies. We *already* have the Spirit, but we do *not yet* see Jesus face to face. Preparing for His return doesn't mean quitting our jobs and sitting on a mountain; it means living with a sense of urgency and faithfulness. It means doing "the Master's business" until He arrives.

Think of it like a surprise party. If you knew your best friend was coming home today, you wouldn't be lazy; you'd be cleaning the house, preparing the food, and watching the window. You'd be excited! If the thought of Jesus returning makes you nervous rather than excited, it's usually because you're holding onto something in this world too tightly. Preparing for Christ's return is about "loosening our grip" on the temporary things of earth so we can reach out for the eternal things of Heaven.

Workbook

Maranatha | Come Quickly, Lord Jesus

1. The "Coming Soon" Paradox Jesus said He was coming "soon" 2,000 years ago.

- ✝ Read **2 Peter 3:8–9**. How does God's view of time differ from ours?

  ____

  ____

- ✝ Why does Peter say God is "slow" in keeping His promise? (Hint: It's about His patience).

  ____

  ____

2. The Readiness Check If Jesus were to return in exactly five minutes, what is the one thing you would be most glad you were doing, and what is the one thing you would be most embarrassed you were doing?

- ✝ **Glad:**

  ____

  ____

- ✝ **Embarrassed:**

  ____

  ____

Heart Check: Longing vs. Fear

- ✝ Does the idea of the world ending scare you?

  ____

  ____

- ✝ How does knowing that the "end of the world" is actually the "beginning of real life" help replace that fear with longing?

  ____

  ____

Mind Map: Traits of the Second Coming

- ✝ **Personal:** It is Jesus Himself, not a representative.
- ✝ **Visible:** Every eye will see Him (Rev 1:7).
- ✝ **Sudden:** Like a thief in the night (1 Thess 5:2).
- ✝ **Triumphant:** He comes as King of kings.

Life Lab: The Window Prayer

The Task: Every morning this week, look out your window at the sky and say, "Maybe today, Lord. Maranatha."

1. Throughout the day, ask yourself: "Would I be okay with Jesus finding me doing this right now?"

    ____

    ____

2. Notice how this shift in perspective changes how you treat people and how you spend your time.

✝ **Observation:**

____

____

____

____

WEEK 48
Expect the Final Judgment

The Big Idea: Accountable

The idea of a "Final Judgment" is one of the most unpopular concepts in modern culture. We like to think of God as a "grandpa in the sky" who ignores our mistakes. But a God without judgment is a God without justice. If God didn't judge evil, it would mean He didn't care about victims, oppression, or sin. The Final Judgment is God's final "Setting Right" of the universe.

For the believer, however, the judgment is different. We must distinguish between the **Great White Throne Judgment** (for those who rejected Christ) and the **Bema Seat of Christ** (for believers).

Because of what we learned in Part 7 (Justification), our *salvation* is not at stake at the Bema Seat. Our "Not Guilty" verdict is already signed in Jesus' blood. Instead, this is a judgment of **Rewards**. Think of it like an awards ceremony after a championship game. Every player on the team gets a ring because they won, but some players receive specific trophies for their effort, their faithfulness, and their sacrifice.

Living with the end in mind means realizing that everything we do matters. Every "secret" act of kindness, every prayer in the closet, and every time you chose integrity over a shortcut is being recorded. God is a generous Paymaster. He doesn't miss a single thing. This shouldn't make us live in a state of constant anxiety, but in a state of **Holy Accountability**. It gives our mundane, daily lives eternal weight. Your life is a "seed" that will produce a specific kind of "harvest" in eternity. When you stand before the Bema Seat, you want to be able to offer Jesus a life that was spent on things that actually last.

Workbook

Accountable | Living with the End in Mind

1. Wood, Hay, and Stubble Read **1 Corinthians 3:11–15**. Paul says our works will be tested by fire.

✝ What kind of works do you think are like "Gold and Silver" (things that survive the fire)?

____

____

✝ What kind of works are like "Wood and Hay" (things that look big but burn up)?

____

____

2. The Motivation Audit We are judged not just on what we did, but *why* we did it.

✝ Have you ever done something "good" just so people would praise you?

____

____

✝ How does knowing Jesus sees your *heart* change how you serve this week?

____

____

Heart Check: The Audience of One

✝ Are you living for the "applause of men" or the "approval of the King"?

____

____

✝ If nobody ever found out about your good deeds, would you still be happy doing them for Jesus' sake?

____

____

Mind Map: What is Judged?

✝ **Our Words:** (Matthew 12:36)

✝ **Our Works:** (2 Corinthians 5:10)

✝ **Our Thoughts/Motives:** (1 Corinthians 4:5)

✝ **Our Stewardship:** (Matthew 25:14-30)

Life Lab: The Eternal Investment

The Task: This week, do one thing that has **zero** benefit for you on earth but is an "investment" in Heaven.

1. It could be giving money anonymously, praying for an enemy, or doing a chore nobody likes.

2. As you do it, say: "This is for the Bema Seat, Lord."

✝ **The Action:**

____

____

✝ **The Internal Feeling:**

____

____

WEEK 49
Look Forward to the New Earth

*"Then I saw "a new heaven and a new earth,"[a] for the
first heaven and the first earth had passed away, and
there was no longer any sea." - Revelation 21:1*

The Big Idea: No More Tears

When most people think of "Heaven," they think of a boring, cloudy place where we float around in white robes playing harps forever. If that sounds unappealing to you, it's because it's not what the Bible promises! Biblical hope isn't about escaping the earth; it's about the **Restoration** of the earth.

Theology calls this the **New Creation**. In Revelation 21 and 22, we see that the story of the Bible ends exactly where it began, in a garden-city where God and man live together. But this time, there is no snake, no sin, and no death. The "New Earth" will be a physical place. We will have physical bodies (like Jesus' resurrection body), we will eat real food, we will work meaningful jobs, and we will explore a universe that is no longer broken by the Fall.

The most beautiful part of this future is the "No More" list. No more cancer. No more depression. No more racism. No more funerals. No more goodbyes. God Himself will "wipe away every tear from their eyes." This isn't just a sentimental thought; it is a promise of total **Reversal**. Every sad thing will come "untrue."

Looking forward to the New Earth changes how we treat the current earth. We don't discard it like a piece of trash; we care for it like a preview of what's to come. We treat our bodies with respect because they are going to be resurrected. We pursue beauty and art because they are echoes of the coming Kingdom. The New Earth is the "Home" our hearts have been homesick for since the day we were born.

Workbook

No More Tears | The World Made New

1. The "No More" List Read **Revelation 21:3–5**. List three things that will be gone forever.

1. ____

2. ____

3. ____

 Which of these are you most excited to see disappear?

____

____

2. The Physical Hope If you could do one thing on a "Perfect Earth" (hike a mountain, paint a sunset, play an instrument) without any pain or frustration, what would it be?

____

____

Heart Check: Homesickness

 Do you ever feel like "something is missing" even when life is going well?

____

____

 How does the promise of the New Earth explain that feeling of "homesickness" for a place you've never been?

____

____

Mind Map: The City of God

 The Light: No need for the sun, for God is its light.

 The Water: The River of the Water of Life.

 The Food: The Tree of Life with twelve kinds of fruit.

 The Gate: Always open; total safety.

Life Lab: The Restoration Vision

The Task: Find something "broken" this week—a piece of nature that's dying, a relationship that's fractured, or even a broken toy.

1. As you look at it, remind yourself: "God is making all things new."

2. Say a prayer of thanks that the "brokenness" of this world is temporary, but the "newness" of the next is eternal.

✝ **What did you look at?**

____

____

____

____

WEEK 50
Live with Eternal Hope

"while we wait for the blessed hope—the appearing of the glory of our great God and Savior, Jesus Christ," -
Titus 2:13

The Big Idea: Future Focus

In the last couple of weeks, we've covered everything from the nature of God to the return of Christ. The question now is: *So what?* How does knowing all this theology change the way you wake up on Monday morning?

Theology calls this **Eternal Hope**. This isn't "hope" in the way the world uses it (like "I hope it doesn't rain"). This is a **Certainty**. It is an anchor for the soul. When you have a "Future Focus," you realize that your current trials are "light and momentary" compared to the weight of glory that is coming (2 Corinthians 4:17).

Imagine you are a runner in a marathon. If you only look at your feet, you will see the blisters, the sweat, and the concrete, and you will want to quit. But if you look at the finish line, if you see the crowd cheering and the medal waiting for you, the pain in your legs doesn't go away, but it becomes *bearable.* You can endure almost anything if you know the ending is good.

Living with eternal hope means you don't have to "get everything you want" right now. You don't have to be the most famous, the richest, or the most successful. You can afford to be generous. You can afford to be patient. You can afford to suffer for the sake of the Gospel because you know your "best life" is yet to come. Today matters forever because today is where we practice the love, the worship, and the character that we will enjoy for trillion upon trillions of years. This isn't the end of the book; it's just the end of the introduction. The real story is about to begin.

Workbook

Future Focus | Why Today Matters Forever

1. The Weight of Glory Read **2 Corinthians 4:16–18**.

✝ Paul calls his immense suffering "light and momentary." How is that possible?

____

____

✝ What "temporary" problem is currently taking up too much space in your mind?

____

____

2. The Anchor How does the "Blessed Hope" (Jesus' return) act as an anchor for you when life feels chaotic?

____

____

Heart Check: The Finish Line

✝ As you finish this chapter, what is the #1 truth that has changed your life the most?

____

____

✝ How are you going to keep your "Future Focus" when the world tries to distract you tomorrow?

____

____

Mind Map: The Fruits of Hope

✝ **Endurance:** The power to keep going.

✝ **Purity:** The desire to be ready for the King.

✝ **Joy:** The ability to smile even through tears.

✝ **Boldness:** The courage to share the Gospel.

Life Lab: The Legacy Letter

The Task: Write a short letter to your "Future Self" (for one year from today).

1. Remind yourself of the hope you found in these 50 weeks.
2. Challenge yourself to keep living for the Audience of One.
3. Seal it and put it in your Bible.

✝ **Date to Open:** _______________________________________

PART TEN
Put Theology to Work

WEEK 51
Apply Theology to Your School Life

"Whatever you do, work at it with all your heart, as working for the Lord, not for human masters," -
Colossians 3:23

The Big Idea: Monday Morning Faith

One of the biggest traps a Christian can fall into is the "Sacred-Secular Divide." This is the idea that God cares about what you do at church or during your private prayer time (the "sacred"), but He doesn't really care about your math homework, your soccer practice, or your lunchroom conversations (the "secular").

Colossians 3:23 shatters that divide. Paul tells us that *whatever* we do, including studying for a chemistry final or writing an essay, is an act of worship if done for the Lord. This means that for a student, "school" is your primary mission field and your primary way to honor God right now. You don't have to wait until you're a "grown-up" to start your ministry. Your ministry is your Monday morning.

Applying theology to school life means three things:

1. **Excellence:** We don't study hard just to get an 'A' or to impress our parents. We study hard because God is a God of order and truth, and by learning about His world, we are honoring Him. Laziness is a poor witness; excellence is a form of praise.

2. **Integrity:** In a world where cheating is common and cutting corners is the norm, a student who lives by the Truth stands out. Theology teaches us that God sees our "secret" life. Integrity means your private character matches your public reputation.

3. **Presence:** You are the "Light of the World" in your hallway. This doesn't mean you have to preach a sermon at the lockers. It means you are the person who sits with the lonely kid at lunch. You are the one who doesn't join in the gossip. You are the one who

handles a bad grade with grace instead of a meltdown.

When you realize that Jesus is your "Teacher" and your "Audience," school stops being a prison and starts being a platform. You aren't just a student; you are an ambassador of the Kingdom of Heaven stationed at a local school.

Workbook

Monday Morning Faith | Doing it All for God

1. The Integration Map Think about your most difficult or "boring" subject in school.

✝ **Subject:** ____

✝ **The "Sacred" View:** How can studying this specific subject actually show you something about God's character? (e.g., Math shows His order; History shows His sovereignty; Science shows His creativity).

____

____

2. The Hallway Witness Identify one "unchristian" norm at your school (e.g., mocking teachers, excluding certain people, obsession with status).

✝ **The Norm:**

____

____

✝ **The Theological Response:** How can you act differently this week based on what you've learned about God's love and justice?

____

____

Heart Check: Who Are You Working For?

✝ When you get a bad grade, do you feel like your "value" has decreased?

____

____

✝ How does the doctrine of Justification (Part 7) protect your heart from the pressure to be perfect at school?

____

____

Mind Map: The Student's Theology

- **Creation:** God made the world we are studying.
- **Fall:** Why school can be frustrating and relationships can be hard.
- **Redemption:** How we bring hope and light into our classrooms.
- **Restoration:** The promise that one day all "unknowing" will be gone.

Life Lab: The Homework Dedication

The Task: Before you start your homework tonight, say a short prayer: "Lord, I offer this work to You. Help me to learn so I can serve others better. May my diligence honor You."

- **Did this change your level of frustration?**

  ____

  ____

- **Did you feel more or less "alone" while studying?**

  ____

  ____

WEEK 52
Share Your Faith with Friends

"But in your hearts revere Christ as Lord. Always be prepared to give an answer to everyone who asks you to give the reason for the hope that you have. But do this with gentleness and respect," - 1 Peter 3:15

The Big Idea: Your Personal Testimony

This is it, the final week. We conclude by looking outward. You have spent a year learning the "Reason for the Hope" that is in you. Now, you must learn how to "make a defense" (the Greek word is ***apologia***, where we get the word "Apologetics").

Apologetics isn't about winning arguments or "smacking" people with Bible verses. Peter tells us two very important things about sharing our faith:

1. **The "Why":** People should *ask* you. This implies that your life is so noticeably full of "hope" that people get curious. If your life looks exactly like the world's, anxious, angry, and hopeless, no one will ever ask you for a reason for your hope.

2. **The "How":** With "gentleness and respect." You are a witness, not a prosecutor. You are sharing a gift, not throwing a rock.

The most effective way to share your faith with friends isn't to memorize a complex philosophical argument (though those are helpful!); it's to share your **Testimony.** Your testimony is simply the story of how God found you and what He is doing in your life. No one can argue with your experience. When you share how Jesus has helped you through anxiety, or how He gave you a sense of purpose, you are making the Gospel "tangible" to your friends. You are inviting them to meet the Person you have come to know over these 52 weeks.

Workbook

Final Project | My Personal Testimony

1. The "Reason for Hope" Draft If a friend asked you today, "Why do you actually believe in God? Is it just because your parents do?", how would you answer in 3-4 sentences using what you've learned this year?

____

____

____

____

____

2. The Personal Story (The "Final Exam")

✝ **The "Before":** One area of my life that was messy or empty before I really understood the Gospel:

____

____

✝ **The "How":** The specific truth about Jesus that changed my perspective (e.g., His grace, His sovereignty, His presence):

____

____

✝ **The "After":** How I handle that same "messy area" differently today because of my faith:

____

____

Heart Check: Gentleness and Respect

✝ Do you ever feel the urge to "win the argument" even if it means losing the friend?

____

____

✝ How can you show "respect" to a friend who completely disagrees with you about God?

____

____

____

Mind Map: Sharing the King

- † **Lifestyle:** Live a life that provokes questions.
- † **Listening:** Earn the right to be heard by listening to their story first.
- † **Language:** Use words they understand (avoid too much "Christianese").
- † **Love:** Stay their friend even if they say "no."

Life Lab: The Prayer of Preparation

The Task: Think of one friend who is far from God.

1. Ask God for a "natural" opportunity to share just one small piece of your story with them this week.

2. Don't force it, wait for the "reason for the hope" moment.

- † **Who are you praying for?**

CONCLUSION
Your Lifelong Path with God

Congratulations. You have completed a 52-week journey through the "Greatest Story Ever Told." But here is the secret: **Theology never ends.** You haven't "finished" learning about God; you have simply built the foundation for a lifetime of discovery. God is infinite, which means there will always be more of His beauty to see, more of His grace to experience, and more of His truth to apply.

As you move forward, remember these three things:

1. **Keep Seeking:** Don't let your Bible become a "dust collector." Keep asking the hard questions. God isn't afraid of your doubts; He wants to meet you in them.

2. **Stay Connected:** You were never meant to walk this path alone. Stay rooted in the Church (Part 8). We need each other to stay on the path.

3. **Trust the Author:** The same God who began this work in you is faithful to complete it (Philippians 1:6). You will have seasons of mountain-top joy and seasons of valley-darkness. In both, the theology you have learned this year will be your anchor.

You are loved by the Father, redeemed by the Son, and empowered by the Spirit. Now, go and live like it.

The End... and the Beginning.

EXTRA CHAPTER
How to Make Systematic Theology Part of Your Everyday Life

"Do not conform to the pattern of this world, but be transformed by the renewing of your mind. Then you will be able to test and approve what God's will is—his good, pleasing and perfect will." - Romans 12:2

The Big Idea: The GPS of the Soul

Let's be real: the phrase "Systematic Theology" sounds like something that belongs in a dusty library with zero Wi-Fi and a lot of old men in elbow patches. But after 52 weeks, you've hopefully realized that theology isn't about memorizing dry facts; it's about building a **worldview.**

Every person on earth has a theology. Every time you say, "That's not fair," you're making a theological statement about justice. Every time you feel like a failure because you didn't get enough "likes," you're following a theology of self-worth. The question isn't *if* you have a theology, but *which* theology is running your life? Systematic theology is simply the "GPS" that helps you navigate the "real world" without crashing into the ditch of hopelessness or the wall of pride.

To make theology part of your everyday life, you have to learn to use it as a **filter**. Before you react to a breakup, a bad grade, or a mean comment, you run it through what you know to be true about God. If you know God is **Sovereign** (Week 5), then a "plan B" in your life isn't a disaster, it's just a detour directed by Him. If you know you are **Justified** (Week 36), then your "mistakes" don't define your identity. Theology takes the "volume" of the world's noise and turns it down so you can hear the truth.

This isn't just about "thinking"; it's about **habits**. You don't have to be a professional theologian to live theologically. You just need to be someone who constantly asks, "How does what I know about God change how I feel about *this*?" Whether you're choosing a college, scrolling through TikTok, or dealing with a family argument, theology is the light that shows you where to step next. It turns a "boring" life into a meaningful mission.

Workbook

The 3 AM Theology Test

1. The Filter Challenge

Take three "common" daily situations and filter them through a specific theological truth you've learned this year.

Situation	Theological Truth (The Lens)	New Perspective
Example: You feel ugly.	**Creation:** I am made in God's image.	My value comes from my Creator, not my mirror.
You get rejected by a friend group.	**Adoption:** (Week 37)	

Situation	Theological Truth (The Lens)	New Perspective
You are terrified of the future.	**Providence:** (Week 6)	
You want to get revenge on someone.	**Total Depravity:** (Week 31)	

2. The "Feed" Filter

Look at the last five posts on your social media feed.

✝ What "theology" (message about God, humans, or happiness) are they preaching?

____

____

✝ How does **biblical theology** counter those messages?

____

____

Heart Check: Head vs. Heart

✝ It's easy to have a "fat head" (lots of knowledge) and a "thin heart" (no love). How can you make sure your study of God makes you more humble and kind rather than more "correct" and arrogant?

____

____

✝ Which attribute of God (from Part 1) do you need to remind yourself of most when you're stressed?

____

____

Mind Map: The Theological Habit Loop

- ✝ **The Trigger:** Something happens (good or bad).
- ✝ **The Pause:** Ask, "What do I know about God that applies here?"
- ✝ **The Response:** Act based on the Truth, not just your feelings.
- ✝ **The Reward:** Peace, perspective, and spiritual growth.

Life Lab: The "Theology Lens" Day

The Task: Tomorrow, pick **one** theological truth (like "God is with me" or "Grace is enough").

1. Write it on your hand or set it as your phone wallpaper.
2. Every time something happens, even something small like a red light or a spilled drink, intentionally apply that truth to the moment.
3. At the end of the day, write down if it changed your stress levels.

- ✝ **The Truth I chose:**

____

____

- ✝ **How it changed my day:**

____

____

Check out another book in the series

Welcome Aboard, Check Out This Limited-Time Free Bonus!

Ahoy, reader! Welcome to the Ahoy Publications family, and thanks for snagging a copy of this book! Since you've chosen to join us on this journey, we'd like to offer you something special.

Check out the link below for a FREE e-book filled with delightful facts about American History.

But that's not all - you'll also have access to our exclusive email list with even more free e-books and insider knowledge. Well, what are ye waiting for? Click the link below to join and set sail toward exciting adventures in American History.

Access your bonus here

https://ahoypublications.com/

Or, Scan the QR code!

www.ingramcontent.com/pod-product-compliance
Lightning Source LLC
Chambersburg PA
CBHW071512140726
47997CB00005B/1947